PLAYBOOK

FOR YOUR EXTRAORDINARY LIFE

TABLE OF CONTENTS

DEDICATION

Every project has a host of people that helped make it happen. In my journey of creating this book, some people were the cheering squad, some applied the grease, some were brave enough to be devil's advocates, and some provided obstacles that, in the end, made the result even better. I can vouch for all of these people having a role in the creation of my own Extraordinary Life.

As I think back, my life has been made better because of all of these folks. Many of them appear in the stories I use to illustrate concepts. Friends, enemies, family, co-workers, professors, significant others...

They have all been my teachers and, for that, I am grateful. Because of them, I am on the path to my Extraordinary Life.

I have had several careers. The first was as a design engineer and then engineering manager. In this career, I experienced firsthand how difficult life could be without any education about how to work with people.

Another of my professions is teaching. As a teacher and coach, I help people improve their personal performance. Personal experience from my 20 years in industry provides a way of thinking about the dynamics of the workplace. When I construct a teaching module, I focus on what it would have taken for me as a technical professional to learn the concept and put it into action.

I use stories and examples when I teach. I hope you choose to learn from these stories as teaching tools instead of considering them an actual recounting of the facts. My stories in this book are as close as I remember, but I have admittedly taken a few liberties to cloud identities. This book is not an autobiography and, in many cases, my sense of what happened is stronger than the details. Hindsight has highlighted what often created a problematic aftermath from my actions and helps me tell the stories in a way that teaches lessons.

My students frequently tell me that they are embarrassed about how they have interacted with others when they understand the implications of their past behaviors. The immediate successes that happen when they use better behaviors and skills often cause regret upon evaluating the damage done and opportunities missed. I tell them to forget their embarrassment about the past because if they had known the correct method all along, they would have been using it. My hope is that you'll recognize where you can learn a better way (or play) and put it into action immediately. No regrets are required.

However, I am sympathetic to their regrets. There are many things I would do differently now that I know how to create success. My own path that has created an Extraordinary Life has made the most progress when I learned to either stop a behavior that was causing problems or I consciously learned how to do and implement a new skill that made life better. These are my plays and I believe they can help you too.

An Extraordinary Life is waiting for you. If the game has been rough, dust yourself off and go back in with these new plays. If you've been waiting on the sidelines, jump in. If you simply want to continue improving your life, good for you. All of us already on the way to an Extraordinary Life are excited for you to join us.

PLAYBOOK

FOR YOUR EXTRAORDINARY LIFE

THE EXTRAORDINARY LIFE

Are you ready to live a life where you:
- Have meaningful relationships that continue to grow?
- Work in a group where interactions actually leave you more energetic instead of sapped?
- See simple, yet elegant, solutions to problems?
- Shine while being who you really are?

If this is the life you want, then you are ready to experience every day as extraordinary. You are ready to live a life beyond what is expected.

Perhaps you feel frustration at being overlooked and not heard when:

AT WORK
- Your boss gives the job you wanted to someone else;
- You can't get the team to see an obvious solution; or
- Everyone seems too busy with their own problems to work together.

AT HOME
- Everything seems to take too much energy and nothing is getting done;
- Your hard work everyday is taken for granted and the chores pile up;
- Everything you say and do seems to be wrong.

IN YOUR PERSONAL LIFE
- You feel treated unfairly or less than someone else;
- There's never enough time and energy for what you love to do;
- There doesn't seem to be a place for you.

If this second set of frustrations with life describes your perspective, then I believe that you are on the path to a life of mediocrity. At some point the struggle to live a life of moving forward against a seemingly overwhelming set of obstacles will wear you down and you'll settle for what ever just happens to come your way.

However, if you intend to live a life that leaves a mark while creating joy and energy, then you are looking to live an Extraordinary LIfe. Living your Extraordinary Life doesn't happen by accident. It is a choice. Extraordinary means remarkable, noteworthy, and beyond what was expected.

THE EXTRAORDINARY LIFE IS ACHIEVED BY:
- The deliberate application of skills for engaging with people in a way they can understand.
- Understanding how people work so you can access creativity on-demand.

This book teaches plays based on researched skills that will keep your light shining. If you are done with being bored or waiting for something to happen, these plays will jumpstart your starring role in an Extraordinary Life.

Many people believe that living an Extraordinary Life can't happen for them. They feel stuck in a struggle to find their place to shine. The opportunity to live an Extraordinary Life seems to be based on magic and chance. It's easy to get caught up in excuses such as only a lucky few folks were in the right place at the right time; had the right family that set them up; were the most gifted in school; or were the fortunate recipient of some other characteristic that is out of our personal control. A uniquely remarkable life seems out of reach. It's just not happening.

Fortunately for us, none of these lucky events matter. Luck and chance are not the ingredients of an Extraordinary Life. There is no magic or serendipity involved in creating the Extraordinary Performance that leads to the Extraordinary Life. The magic is actually an outcome. It is what happens when you put the plays into action. The plays that create this life can be learned by everyone if they can find a teacher. I'm offering to be that teacher for you. You can do it once you learn the plays.

During the past 20 years I have taught Leadership skills to several thousand students. I have personally coached hundreds of people, from those just beginning their career to seasoned executives. As I have learned more about what creates remarkable performance, my undergrad and adult students frequently give me feedback that what I teach has changed their lives. Recently, my students and coachees have asked *Have you written a book so I can read about this? I can't take notes fast enough!*

So, this is that book. It is a how-to guide of Plays that will lead you to an Extraordinary Life. The Plays are deliberate skills and actions. When the Plays are used to tap into your creativity, build long-term positive relationships, and engage groups to have an impact, Extraordinary Performance happens. And when you are living this life of remarkable performance, you are on the way to an Extraordinary Life.

This book is a collection of the recurring techniques and perspectives I teach others. My coaching conversations start with work scenarios, but we always end up talking about how to apply the plays with friends and family.

It is heartwarming to experience how much people care about friends and family. It is a clear priority for everyone I teach and coach. These techniques work equally well at home and work.

Ah-Ha! moments happened for me as I began a formal study of how people perform at their best. The researchers would explain the science of performance and I would suddenly have an explanation for a personal experience from my life at work or home. Situations that had always been a mystery to me, became clear. Immediately, I understood why someone had unexpectedly become angry, why my feelings were hurt, or I didn't get the job opportunities I felt I deserved. I understood why some days I was creative and other days I accomplished very little. I also realized that my life would have been better if I had known the things I was just now learning as an over-40 adult. Over and over I thought *Why didn't someone teach me this when I was 20? It would have kept me from burning so many bridges in my attempts to be a success. Wow, I could have accomplished so much more with my work and had a great time making friends along the way.* I felt I had been so close to making a big impact, and had barely missed the mark when it came to creating the remarkable.

In my coaching, I find that most people need education on the same of set of skills I needed. Just like we all need to know basic math if only to exchange money for goods, we all need a basic set of skills for working with each other. Math classes start on the first day of school. Somehow, the classes about working with each other are left out. Even though we are all unique, there is a common set of difficulties that hold us back and we need a common skillset for handling them. My recurring coaching conversations about understanding people, handling adversities, and being creative are the plays in this book.

Accessing Extraordinary Performance on-demand instead of accidently requires understanding key insights about how the brain embraces ideas, how-to's for methodically engaging with others for positive outcomes, and different ways of thinking about your everyday life. These skills and perspectives are the plays in this playbook that can be used to create a life exceptional in character, amount, and degree. An experience that is truly remarkable...your Extraordinary Life.

MY PERSPECTIVE

Until 1994 when I began my journey of learning the plays that create an Extraordinary Life, I believed that these skills were a gift that some people had and others didn't...and I was one of the have-nots. It was clear to me that although I was very good at getting things done, I was not good at getting things done in a way that built and maintained relationships. I was a creative, technical expert when it came to engineering, but desperately lacked the skills for working with people. I was certain that getting along with others wasn't one of my abilities.

For me, dealing with people felt a lot like trying to pick up a chainsaw that was on the ground running at full speed, bouncing wildly. I dreaded interacting with others because I knew it would only bring trouble. It seemed risky and dangerous with unpredictable results. Whatever I said or did resulted in somebody taking it wrong. I was constantly wasting time and energy with my unsuccessful dance around emotions and other agendas. In hindsight, I worked with a wonderful set of people who had all the usual troubles and complaints – along with kindness and a sense of wanting to get the job done. The problem was me. My perspective and lack of skills for working with people made me the difficult one.

I found my company's standard training classes on communication and conflict incredibly interesting, but when I returned to work and home, I didn't change a thing. I had not internalized how to use the information. At the conclusion of one training class in communication, I asked the instructor, "I really enjoyed all these games and the class, but what do I do with this when I get back to work?" She told me to just talk with people and it would be OK. I couldn't believe her advice. My response was, "They already spend too much time talking about their kids, fishing, and football. No way am I going to encourage more wasted time!"

I couldn't translate the classes into practice. I simply did not understand what to do. Using people skills had no basic operational plan, and even worse, wasn't focused on getting the job done. The turning point came for me in a graduate-level counseling psychology class where one session was devoted to learning a fundamental technique for drawing people out. (The technique is commonly called Active Listening. My version of this technique is the play for Dynamic Listening™ in the section Building Positive Relationships.) It was a very brief exercise, but along with learning the technique, I received a flash of insight. I discovered there were rules and formulas for how to talk with people. I realized that the training classes I had previously attended did not break communication into to specific steps and words, and I needed steps. Now I had a formula of what to say with specific words to use. I was so excited!

As unbelievable as it may sound, this one class changed my life. This insight of using formulas and details for working with others is what drives my teaching. I believe that people need to know exactly what to do, practice it, and then once the basics are working, they can begin to improvise to fit their personality. I needed a Playbook and I believe that most other people need it too. That very night I started my quest to learn the rules and formulas that would take me from being a technical expert who was limited by her ability to build synergy with others to a life of Extraordinary Performance.

The plays in this book are the rules, formulas, and ways of thinking that have helped me move from struggling to work with my family, friends, and colleagues to creating Extraordinary Performance and an Extraordinary Life. These plays have helped my students and coachees. I know they will help you too.

THE PLAYBOOK

FUNDAMENTALS & GENERAL RULES

An Extraordinary Life with Extraordinary Performance is a life that is beyond what is expected and usual. This collection of plays enables you to change your thinking about everyday interactions so you can deliberately design actions that create the remarkable. You might think that a remarkable life is only for the lucky. Luckily for all of us, it can be deliberately designed and executed.

THE GAME OF EXTRAORDINARY

Thinking about working with others as a game with plays can sound off-putting, as if what you do regarding your life really doesn't matter since it is just a game. Or perhaps it sounds manipulative to plan out plays to get what you want.

My notion of using plays for working with others simply means that you have choices about how to engage. Many of my examples are about myself where I describe my own bad behavior. My problem was that I didn't know I had choices about how to engage and I had never learned options. I only knew one way to engage. For instance, in an on-going argument over work priority, I was a bully. I didn't know my choices were (1) to continue arguing; or (2) attempt to understand other people's needs and the needs of the group regarding the use of resources to work things out; or (3) keep a record of what was happening so that our management could decide how the resources should be used. Each of these actions was a choice, and now I see them as my plays. This playbook provides you with choices so you can work with others in ways that they understand.

So, this collection of plays is a playbook for how to create the Extraordinary Performance that results in an Extraordinary Life. Most of us behave in ways based on what we saw as children or perhaps we learned from someone we admired. We mimic how someone else handled a situation without even thinking about it. Our actions seem like the thing to do because we have been unconsciously programmed to use those responses. And once we have been successful using a play, we are not likely to give it up – even when it is not working very well. It has become our only option unless we deliberately choose something else.

Gaming life and gaming the system imply taking unfair advantage. The Extraordinary Life would never purposefully make unfair or unethical choices. Using a playbook for creating the remarkable provides the choices and freedom to try a play. Then, if things don't go as expected, you can try something different.

Looking at life every day as a game in which you have choices of what to do and how to accomplish your goal creates enthusiasm, levity, and freedom to try new techniques and learn new skills. These plays offer you deliberate choices and strategies.

SCRIPTS FOR EFFICIENCY

One of the most daunting parts of attacking the obstacles that keep you from an Extraordinary Life is the work it takes to get plays so familiar that they are automatic responses. However, practicing good plays until they are automatic is crucial because it is completely overwhelming to approach every situation from a clean page. There is not enough time to come up with a new way to handle everything that comes your way.

The good news is that once you develop the play for a particular situation, you can simply call it back up every time that situation occurs. The plays become scripts where you know your lines and responses. As you use a play and receive feedback based on how people respond, you will hone your scripts to be efficient and effective.

Several years ago I was coaching young supervisors in a manufacturing company. These rookie managers had little training in management and leadership techniques. They had primarily been promoted because they were great at getting things done and proactive when unexpected barriers were encountered.

John was one of the young men I was coaching. He was known for taking charge and getting something done when there were problems in his area. His technique was to look at the situation, jump to a conclusion of what was wrong, and then fire off a solution. He admitted that sometimes the results were spectacular, but sometimes he totally missed the problem and an effective solution. I talked with him about how the research described him perfectly. The natural tendency of most people is to select the first reasonable solution that comes to mind in an effort to do away with the problem. We discussed a plan where he would have a rule to always get three solutions or iterations on what seemed to be a good solution. Then I coached him on how to solicit ideas from his team and to insist that they always generate at least three alternatives before choosing the next step.

It was not clear to me that John embraced my coaching until we talked two months later. In our session John told me, "I wasn't sure about taking the time to get three alternatives, but then I noticed that when my Department Superintendent calls us in to talk about a problem, he always insists we come up with three ideas before we choose one. The group always wants to jump up and execute the first idea presented, but he forces us to come up with three. Over and over, I see that you are right – the ideas just build off of each other. The first one is never what we really need to do."

John also discovered that he did not need a new play for every time his group needed to problem-solve a solution. Instead, he only needed to call up his *Let's get three alternatives* script.

New managers can become overloaded quickly. They often become bogged down trying to figure out what to do in what appears to be a novel situation to them, but is actually a standard problem supervisors face. It frequently looks like they do not know what they are doing. They probably don't. New managers do not have their playbook of scripts that let them efficiently deal with the repetitive problems and scenarios they face. Experienced managers avoid putting a lot of time or energy into repetitive scenarios because they have a finely tuned script that is called up out of their playbook.

Whether you are a manager, parent, or a person focused on creating a new future, as you use these plays you will develop and hone proven scripts and habits that allow you to move toward Extraordinary Performance using your Playbook of proven techniques.

ELAINE'S LAW OF EIGHT PERCENT (8%)

If you were in my physical classroom, you would see me make a half-circle motion with my arms to illustrate many different points. This motion helps my students visualize the different parts of a whole. Elaine's Law of 8% is best explained by this visual. Elaine's Law of 8% says that in every group, about 8% of the people are focused on different goals and cause problems for the rest. Nothing works when it comes to getting the 8% to improve.

When talking about the 8%, I use a 180° semi-circle to represent the whole group. This group can be your whole team, your entire organization, your whole department, or your whole family. It's everybody, for however you define the whole, for a particular scenario.

From my experience with groups, about 92% of my half-circle represents good people that came to play. These folks have good intentions. They want

THE WHOLE

THE 92%

THE 8%

to do good work and they intend to be successful. They are doing their best to create their own extraordinary life. Then there is the other part of the half-circle – the 8%. My sense is that about 8% of any group has a different agenda and causes trouble for the 92% that came to play. When I work with student teams, for every 100 students there are 5 to 10 troublemakers, for an average of about 8%. In the section *A How-To Guide for Changing Yourself*, I tell a story about a fellow named Steve. He was one troublemaker in a group of about 12 people. It seems that the 8% are focused on something different than the objective of the group.

Here is a key concept about using these plays. DO NOT ATTEMPT these on the 8%. The plays will not work. These plays only work on the 92%, the folks that came to engage. When you use these plays with the 92%, you will be amazed at the quick response and remarkable things that start to happen.

However, the 8% are so troublesome and difficult to handle that they get most of the attention. You will think *Maybe this play will get ol' so-and-so to straighten up!* Unfortunately, the 8% are a black cloud over the other players. If you use these plays on them, the plays will not work and you will decide that these techniques are worthless. Nothing works on the 8%. Your best bet is to find a way to keep them from harassing and keeping everyone else from being exceptional.

THE FUNDAMENTALS

Whether I am coaching an individual in-person or teaching a group in a classroom setting, my goal is to help people understand a concept and then deliberately design the steps to put it into action. I believe that Extraordinary Performance depends on taking action. The process starts with learning about the skills. The process works when the educational process of learning about a topic moves forward to putting skills into practice.

The first fundamental practice you'll need to use these plays is a method for actively putting a new skill into practice or eliminating a habit that is not getting you what you want. The section *A How-To Guide for Changing Yourself* provides a methodology to guide your personal change process. In this chapter you will learn how to internalize and practice a new play so that it becomes your natural way of doing things. You will need this way of thinking and knowledge about yourself as the base skill for moving from reading about the plays to actually playing the game.

I have found the best leverage for getting folks on board with improving is to actually let them know what they need to work on. It might sound simplistic, and most people believe that they know what they do well and what they are not so good at. But, a fresh look at themselves from the perspective of those that know them and are subjected to working and living with them is a real attention-getter.

Thus, the second fundamental practice is for you to identify the skills you do well and those that need improvement. The way to get this feedback is by using a 360-survey. You will find this survey tool at the conclusion of the book in the section – Using the Ambio360™. This online survey provides feedback on how you stack up against the top skills that are reported to Need Work. Getting feedback about yourself isn't one of the plays, but it lets you know what you do well and shines a light on your blind-spots. Using the survey is not difficult. Summoning up a big dose of courage to be able to see yourself the way everyone else does is the hard part.

HOW TO USE THIS BOOK

This book is organized into distinct sections of stand-alone topics. I encourage you to think about the topics as plays in your playbook for Extraordinary Performance. This guide starts with a section on fundamental skills that are building blocks to be used in working with people. Many of the plays are ideas I use when coaching people. I believe you can use these plays to improve your skills and develop a strategy for working with others.

THE PLAYS

The remainder of the book provides methodology and how-to guides for tapping into your creativity on demand, creating relationships, deliberately acting in a way that results in Extraordinary Performance, and providing the extra sauce to bring about change.

THE PLAYS ARE COLLECTED IN CATEGORIES FOR:
- Building Positive Relationships
- The Math of Extraordinary
- Creating Extraordinary Performance
- Harnessing Your Horsepower

Although you can read the Sections and Plays in any order, the book makes the most sense if you read it sequentially from start to finish. The plays often refer to a previously discussed skill or example, and will make more sense when you have the background.

A HOW-TO GUIDE FOR CHANGING YOURSELF

You are faced with an important choice. You can:
- Read this book as an academic exercise, or
- Actively put these plays into practice.

If your choice is to simply read, then enjoy the stories and thinking about the plays. My experience says you'll change anyway. Even if you believe you don't need to change, when you find yourself in a spot that could use the plays, your subconscious will prod you with a *Why not? I can do this a better way!* If your choice is to start using these plays to create the Extraordinary Performance that leads to your Extraordinary Life, then the first step is to learn how you change yourself.

When it comes to personal improvement, there's a methodology for putting the plays into practice. The methodology depends on your willingness to become an expert detective. Putting a new play into action requires that you become completely aware of what is going on so the light bulb can go off to remind you that you have a new tool to use. Success at changing your responses (using a new play) starts with your analysis of what is going on so you know when you could put your new play into action. You'll need to do some forensic analysis by treating your life like a crime scene to understand what the environment looks, feels, and smells like when you need your new play. When you understand what to watch for, you'll recognize a specific signal that lets you know that you have a new play to use. Your first step is to figure out when you are *fixin' to* need your new play. *Fixin' to* is an East Tennessee way to say it's about to happen, i.e. *It's fixin' to* rain. The second step is, once you have identified the *fixin' to* signal, you stop what you usually do and call up your new, improved skill.

THE SKEET SHOOTER

The methodology for changing can be understood from two examples from my personal experiences when I first embarked on deliberately improving. Many years ago I was in my office one afternoon when the phone rang. The caller never identified himself, but he asked me if I was a sports psychologist, and I confirmed that I have a Ph.D. in sport psychology. He told me one of his friends had heard about me and recommended that he give me a call. I was curious as to what this was all about so I asked him to continue. This gentleman told me he was a championship skeet shooter, and the conversation went like this:

SKEET SHOOTER: Do you know anything about skeet shooting?
ELAINE: Not a thing.
SKEET SHOOTER: Do you have any questions?
ELAINE: So, how good are you?
SKEET SHOOTER: I'm in the top five in the state.
ELAINE: Are they hard to hit?
SKEET SHOOTER: No, they are easy to hit.
ELAINE: How many do you miss?
SKEET SHOOTER: A round is 100 clay pigeons. I don't know how many I miss...it varies...maybe two or three or five or only two... I don't know.
ELAINE: Which ones do you miss?
SKEET SHOOTER: I miss number 22, 51, 25, 42, 76...I don't know, I just miss.
ELAINE: If they are easy to hit why do you miss?
SKEET SHOOTER: I miss because it is difficult to focus long enough to hit 100. It's boring and you can't focus that long.
ELAINE: (At this point I thought to myself...if it is so boring why do you do it? But, I kept my thoughts to myself)
SKEET SHOOTER: I could lay 100 clay pigeons on the ground in a row and give you a hammer and ask you to break all of them in order. You would miss one before you broke all 100. It's hard to focus long enough to hit a hundred.

We talked on for a bit and I recommended that he dress in his skeet shooting gear, go with a friend to the range, and shoot several rounds as if he were in a match. It seemed to me that there was no apparent pattern to the misses and the problem was one of maintaining focus on what he wanted to do. So, during these rounds that simulated a live match, I asked him to pay attention to what he was thinking about or what was going on in the surroundings when he did miss. Once he uncovered a common signal that was associated with a miss, he would know his *fixin' to*. Then he could preload his subconscious with the signal was that he was *fixin' to* miss so he could re-focus on his shooting. In other words, his internal dialogue would go like this:

INTERNAL COACH: Hey! You are distracted and *fixin' to* miss! Focus on your shooting!
SKEET SHOOTER: Thanks! I got it and am re-focused on my shooting!

The gentleman stated that he did not think this solution would help him and hung up the phone. I thought to myself, Well, I guess you get what you pay for, and I did not think much more about it.

About three months later he called me back. He was ecstatic because his shooting had greatly improved and he had done well over the weekend. He explained that after our chat, he had not found any better ideas, so he went to the range and did as I suggested. He discovered that during his test rounds of shooting 100 clay pigeons he would begin to notice his gun, how the gun felt in his hands, and the sun shining on the gun barrel. When his focus shifted to his gun he would miss.

His solution was to preload his subconscious mind to watch for when he was *fixin' to* miss. His signal was when he started to notice his gun. When his subconscious mind sensed the signal, it would remind him to refocus his shooting. His signal that he was *fixin' to* was noticing his gun and his new play was to refocus on skeet shooting when he saw that signal.

SMELLING LIKE A SKUNK

You may be thinking, I'm not a skeet shooter and I'm not interested in athletic performance. So, the following story is about me. I would be uncomfortable telling this tale on myself, except that at the time I did not know any other way to handle this problem. I didn't have any plays except what I had seen, and I had only seen winning by being intimidating through having more data, being quicker on my feet with verbal comebacks, and being smarter from having done more homework – somewhat of a bully. Rather than be embarrassed about my behavior, I am proud of having the courage to try something different. I believe the first few times you try a new response, you will discover just how much courage it takes. So, this example relates how I used my technique to modify my behavior in an unpleasant, ongoing workplace scenario.

As an engineering manager, I supervised a small group of people that used a shared group of computers to do their graphic analysis work. These computers ranged in computational horsepower from several small computers for doing initial layouts to a few medium horsepower computers for inputting graphics and setting up computations. And then there was the big machine. It was a beauty in graphic presentation with the equivalent of a High Definition display back in the 1990's. It also had plenty of horsepower for doing deluxe computations. At the time, this expensive machine was a specialty and it would be programmed to crunch numbers all night or perhaps all weekend for large, complex simulations of engineering designs for our manufacturing process.

Almost everyone that used these shared resources got along well, and the group self-managed who needed to work on which machines in order to get all of their tasks accomplished. The almost everyone was because of one user – Steve. Steve worked for a research group and reported to a different supervisor. He seemed to believe that whatever work he was doing was more important than the work of other folks, and refused to collaborate on how to use the limited resources to best achieve everyone's scheduled deliverable dates.

Regularly, one of my employees would come to my office to let me know that Steve was camped out on the deluxe computer and would not work out a schedule. I would jump up from my chair, run down the steps to the computer room, and confront Steve. Our conversation would be unpleasant and we never reached any sort of agreeable conclusion. After this went on for several months, one of my colleagues called me aside and said, "Everybody knows Steve is not working well with your team. We all have problems working with Steve. However, you are starting to be known for fighting. It doesn't matter whether you are right or not, as the old saying goes *If you get in a pissin' contest with a skunk, both you and the skunk stink at the end of it. I just want you to know you are starting to stink.*"

I found this feedback quite upsetting, because my intention was not to be difficult with anyone, and I for sure did not want a reputation of being adversarial. My motivation was completely on getting the work done. I vowed to myself that I would no longer fight with Steve.

ROUND 1: Started that afternoon when my employees showed up again to complain about Steve. As usual, I jumped up from my desk, ran to the computer room, and let Steve have it. About two hours later as I was walking to a meeting, it hit me that I had once again done the very thing that was *fixin' to* cause me trouble. Again, I resolved that I would no longer fight with Steve.

ROUND 2: Began the next morning when the team showed up to let me know of their troubles with Steve. This time I saw the signal that I was *fixin' to* do something that was not going to end well. I hung my head at the daunting task ahead as I walked to the computer room and into the cubicle where Steve sat at the computer. I just stood there. I had no plan of what to do. I only knew my old way of dealing with the situation. So, I literally just stood there. I had nothing to say except the usual inflammatory language, and I had vowed to myself not to use those words again. Steve proceeded to start with his side of the usual defensive dialogue, and I just stood there saying nothing. Finally, I turned and walked away because I had no better plan. But, at least I had not added fuel to the fire.

I returned to my office, closed the door, sat at my desk and proceeded to write out a short script of what I wanted to say. I had no experience in how to work successfully with someone like Steve. I only knew to push back when pushed. It took me well over an hour to come up with a simple script to explore Steve's needs in an attempt to work something out to use the resources effectively with the entire group. With my door shut, I stood in the middle of my office and read my script out loud until I had it memorized. It was a difficult chore to get the words out because it was a way of interacting that I had only read about and never put into practice.

ROUND 3: Started the next morning when the team came to let me know they were again having difficulty with Steve. There was no jumping up and running to confront him. I walked to the computer room as if facing the hangman. This was not my usual style and the words I had memorized did not come naturally. I was convinced that I was about to look foolish. I walked into Steve's cubicle and asked if we could talk about his assigned tasks and priorities so that the resource could be managed for everyone to get their work done.

Steve never heard my new language. His signal was that when Elaine appeared, she had come to fight. I appeared and, right on cue, he started the same old defensive argument. I had programmed Steve to behave this way through my persistent poking at him. I went back to my office, started taking notes about our troubles and documenting what was going on. I was never able to work it out with Steve, but I quit my side of the fight and stopped the damage to my reputation. My signal was any time I had to approach Steve regarding resources I was *fixin' to* do something that was not helpful and could potentially be damaging to my career and ability to make an impact.

I'd like to tell you that my new strategy repaired our relationship and Steve and I became great friends. Or at a minimum, that Steve and I were able to work things out in the future. The truth of the matter is that Steve and I never did work things out. But, I found a new way to work on the issue that eventually led to someone with more clout getting the situation resolved. I started running a new play and have kept it in my playbook ever since.

3-STEP METHODOLOGY FOR IMPLEMENTING PERSONAL CHANGE

The formula for change is simple in principle. The difficulty comes when you are asked to respond differently to a signal. It is an easy change to try out a new route to work because it is not personal and we can evaluate the potential hazards. When we attempt a new behavior, it usually feels like we are admitting to a personal flaw. We feel exposed and potentially at risk from appearing differently in our world. It's not a step, but the first thing you'll need is a dose of courage to admit there is a better way and it's time you used it.

STEP 1: You identify a habit you want to change or a new skill you want to put into practice.

STEP 2: You engage in detective work to figure out the signal that you are *fixin' to* engage in a troublesome habit OR you have a new play to use.

Signals can be an actual scenario, as in my example with Steve. I knew that every time I had to approach Steve in the computer room, I was *fixin' to* get in trouble.

Signals also manifest as a particular feeling or emotional trigger. In the example of the Skeet Shooter, his signal was noticing his gun, how the light reflected on his gun, or how the gun felt in his hands.

For instance, you might notice a feeling of needing to be in a hurry just before interrupting someone, or a feeling of irritation when you are in the middle of a task and a colleague stops by to ask a question. A specific environment, a particular person, a weekly meeting, or a feeling in your body can provide you with important information. It can be a signal that acts as a STOP sign. The signal triggers you to stop what you are doing because you have learned a better response.

Identifying your signal and deliberately preloading it into your subconscious is a key step. Once you are engaging in your old response, it is too late. You are in motion and it is unlikely you can hear your little voice that says *You are fixin' to regret this.* The goal is that when the signal happens, you Stop. Then Step 3 kicks in with a new response.

STEP 3: You determine a new reaction to the signal. Most of the time, the reaction is two-fold with the first reaction being to just stop, especially in emotionally charged situations. When the signal is an emotion or feeling, the first response is to stop your train before the wreck happens. Then you can recall your specific plan of what to do next.

In the case of implementing a new skill, once Step 2 has recognized the signal, whether an emotion or a scenario, you implement your new play. It is impossible to determine your new response when you are in the midst of being triggered. You will need to spend some time up front to deliberately plan your new action and attach it to the trigger. If your new action requires a different way of talking to someone or asking questions, you'll want to write out your response and then actually say the script out loud. Writing something down is a very different action than talking, and in the heat of a situation, it is just about impossible to speak a new script. Closing your door and practicing new scripts sounds simple, but it is a requirement for you to be speaking the new words when you see the signal.

BUILDING POSITIVE RELATIONSHIPS

PLAY #1
COMMUNICATION BASICS

PLAY #2
DYNAMIC LISTENING

PLAY #3
CURIOSITY AND THE ART OF POSITIVITY

PLAY #4
GIVING ADVICE

PLAY #5
FYI: FI'S VS. FD'S

PLAY #1
COMMUNICATION BASICS

If you asked me to sum up this book, my answer would be, "This book teaches you how to build positive relationships. How you interact with others and how you decide to interpret life is the foundation of relationships. Once the skills of building positive relationships become part of your daily habits, your Extraordinary Life will start to unfold."

Positive relationships are those that leave you feeling energized after contact with a person. Even if the topic is unpleasant, the interaction itself leaves you with more energy. Research on the effect of positive relationships is extensive. There are clear conclusions that have been consistently repeated. For instance:

- Do you want to be healthier? People with positive relationships recover faster from surgery, have fewer significant illnesses and fewer minor illnesses, and their life expectancy is longer.

- Would you like to hone your skills to become an important player at work, home, sport, or play? People in positive relationships demonstrate improved focus on what they are doing. Their positive relationships provide a safety net that allows them to focus on what they are trying to achieve. This safety net helps to eliminate the anxiety and worry associated with difficult and negative situations and a fear of failure.

- Do you want to be more creative? Then build a network of supportive people and positive relationships. Relationships built on a history of positivity provide the benefit of the doubt when disagreements occur. Positive relationships create a sense that things can be worked out instead of starting with a baseline expectation that amenable solutions won't happen. With positive relationships, more ideas are exchanged with an increased willingness to work together, resulting in creating more value. The accumulation of positive interactions is the key to opening the door to possibilities.

THE IMPORTANCE OF COMMUNICATION SKILLS

Communication skills are the cornerstone of positive relationships. These skills are not plays, but instead are basic skills you will need to master and use in almost every play. Just like blocking is a skill in football that is integral to both offensive and defensive plays, communication skills are basic to the plays for Extraordinary Performance.

Research is clear that communication skills are perhaps the most important for successfully working with people. However, when people are asked to evaluate their own personal communication skills, the overwhelming response is *My communication skills are great. It is other people that have the problems. Not me.* Thus, the first problem with teaching these skills is that people don't think they need improvement. They listen with an ear that is tuned to pointing out how others need the skills instead of internalizing how they can improve.

Whether you believe you need to work on your communication skills or not, when it comes to the basics, it never hurts to hone them. Just like the professional athlete who continues to practice the basics every day to become better and better, I encourage you to keep working on your communication skills to achieve mastery.

Insights from communication research construct a compelling argument for mastering communication skills:

- In studies of performance in companies and organizations, communication problems are overwhelmingly identified as the primary obstacle to performance. Having the smartest employees, the latest technology or the best product does not guarantee success. The inability to communicate with each other effectively is the key problem.
- When it comes to being promoted, a top-10 criteria is the ability to communicate face-to-face. Unfortunately, per recent research, as a person's use of emails and texts goes up, their interpersonal skill level goes down.

Most people strive for promotion as they gain experience. Some people want to move into a management career with the goal of managing people to create a successful business. Some people want to move up a technical or discipline career ladder where they have influence over the products or projects in an organization. To be recognized as competent to lead others as a technical expert or a manager, interpersonal skills of communicating and listening are consistently rated as the most important.

A HOW-TO FOR BEING COMPASSIONATE

The importance of communication skills as a foundation became clear to me one Sunday morning. I attend a small, 25-member Methodist church in my mountain community of upper Cosby. When our pastor is away, I am one of the designated speakers. My strategy for developing a sermon is to open up my management textbook and choose a topic on how to engage with people in a way that creates value. After years of teaching these topics, I understand the principles and have real-life examples. Once I find the topic, I turn to the Internet and search for supporting scriptures and religious thinking. I usually offer thoughts on how to live better, and how the topic fits with our spiritual lives.

In preparation for one of these Sunday sermons, my management handbook seemed to open itself to a discussion of compassion. In the business world, research is clear that organizations demonstrating compassion have improved outcomes from their employees. Surely, I thought, compassion would be a safe topic for discussion in a religious forum. Little did I know that the big lesson would be a personal one for me.

Being compassionate means that you are willing to share suffering. I thought I was a compassionate person. I am tender-hearted and try to jump in and help when people have trouble or I just think they might have trouble. What I found was that I was only two-thirds compassionate. I had been running away from the other third that depends on a foundation of communication skills.

Being compassionate has three steps:

STEP 1: Recognize suffering or that a circumstance has occurred where
           someone might be suffering.
STEP 2: Connect with the person about the suffering...
           share the feeling...be empathetic.
STEP 3: Take action to help relieve the suffering.

When I evaluated my performance on these three steps, I discovered that I came up short on Step 2. Even worse, I felt a knot in my belly at the very thought of having to connect with someone who was suffering. I had been taking the easy way out although I tried to be aware of suffering or the potential for suffering. When I knew of suffering, I would usually take physical action such as fixing the problem, sending help or contributing funds, but I was leaving out Step 2 - Connecting. It felt too risky. I had rationalized that my role was to help behind the scenes and it was someone else's job to connect.

Luckily for me, realizing I was leaving out this step led me to a well-used play that would help with Step 2. I simply needed the signal to use it. The play for connecting is Dynamic Listening™, and it follows in this section. In fact, Dynamic Listening is where I first understood that the plays are not magic. They are very deliberate and have a structure. My signal is when I start to say, "How can I help?" to someone in a bad spot, I also connect at an emotional and personal level.

THE LIE ABOUT SUCCESS

The myth we are taught is that if you work hard, good things will happen. You will get promoted. In fact, the myth extends with the proposition that those who are the smartest in their field and/or work the hardest will rise to the top. These lies are easy to believe because both of them are entirely within your personal control. You can choose to work long hours and stay hyper-organized. You can choose to focus on your discipline and become an expert.

The truth about personal success is that one-half is working hard and knowing your discipline. The other half is the ability to use the first half while engaging with other people. The half that is engaging with people can feel out of control because there is no clear standard for evaluating what a feeling is. It is always risky engaging with people. An individual's response can be unpredictable based on their perspective or simply from an emotional interaction that occurred right before you approached them. Working with people feels uncertain, and that's why it takes courage to engage. You can follow all the rules, have good intentions, and still get burned. However, the formulas for engaging are your only hope for creating positive relationships – the key ingredient for an Extraordinary Life.

RELATIONSHIP KILLERS

John Gottman spent his career analyzing relationships. Dr. Gottman is famous for developing his research to the point of being able to predict the long-term success or failure of a relationship with 94% accuracy by watching the first three minutes of a couple's discussion about something where they have a disagreement. The disagreeable topic can appear to be only a small sticking point. The problem is not measured by the scale of the argument or the outrage from an angry person.The key ingredient that predicts long-term relationships is if the couple is able to repair their relationship when having a disagreement or when regrettable events happen.

Dr. Gottman zeroed in on four top relationship killers that show up in how we communicate with each other. Actions which are death to relationships are:

CRITICISM

Feedback is a good thing. Letting someone know that something is a problem for you is healthy. It is information to help someone improve.

Criticism is not feedback. It implies to another person that they are not OK at their very foundation. Criticism sounds like you, as in you never..., you always..., how could you..., and my favorite *Do whatever you want, that's what you always do anyway.*

DEFENSIVENESS

The easiest way to recognize defensiveness is when a person starts making excuses because of a perception of unfair treatment. Although it might not be verbalized, the message is: It's not my fault. *Well, I didn't call the plumber because I was busy with the end of month reports. You know the last week of the month is always a killer for me! Plus, it's not an emergency anyway. A little leak will wait a few days.*

If you are under attack, you must defend yourself. Defending yourself is not being defensive. A healthy exchange would sound like *I knew I had a busy week. I should have asked you to make the call. It's after hours now – Would you be able to call tomorrow? My whole week is packed with end of month reports.*

STONEWALLING

Stonewalling is shutting down and not engaging. The listener does not give either verbal or non-verbal signals that they are tracking the conversation. When the topic requires a decision or discussion about a difficult topic, stonewalling happens when a person gets busy with something else or tunes out to avoid engaging. The stonewaller comes across as having hunkered down at worst, or at the least, not caring.

Stonewalling breaks down relationships because it wears out the other parties. It takes too much effort to push on a stonewaller to engage, and eventually, the other side will simply take action or walk away. Dealing with a stonewaller feels like pushing a rope.

CONTEMPT

Contempt is the worst of the relationship killers. Contempt tells the other side *You are not worth this discussion and I don't care.* Contempt is disrespectful of the other person and attempts to ridicule the other side to affect their behavior. Contempt implies *You are simply not good enough and a waste of my time.*

Do you kill relationships on purpose? Probably not, especially with all those people who came to make a difference and are working on their own versions of an Extraordinary Life. If your relationships with people seem to often be difficult, perhaps these four relationship killers are to blame.

The relationship death process starts with our small responses to everyday life that are instances of Criticism, Defensiveness, Stonewalling, and Contempt. These little negative actions are stones that begin to pile up and eventually build a wall. It takes daily attention to keep the stones out of your relationship pathways.

The plays in this section specifically offer ways to engage that build relationships. The plays are not tactics to avoid killing relationships. Actually, the plays are positive ways to say what you need to say and engage in a way so that people want to work with you. In fact, much of this book can be traced back to specific behaviors or ways of thinking that offer relationship builders instead of relationship killers.

POSITIVE RELATIONSHIP PLAYS

The plays in the Positive Relationship section of the Playbook focus on communication skills, how to get information, and how to improve the quality of engagement with other people.

DYNAMIC LISTENING™ – teaches a basic foundation skill for talking about what is going on and how people feel about it.

CURIOSITY – and the Art of Positivity is a play that helps you to create a mindset focused on possibilities.

GIVING ADVICE – is a play for helping others evaluate their options and create an action plan for moving forward.

FYI: FI'S VS. FD'S – is a play that helps expand your communication style to understand your own focus while accommodating all kinds of listeners.

PLAY #2

DYNAMIC LISTENING™

Dynamic Listening™ sounds like an oxymoron. Dynamic means exciting, and most of us believe listening is boring and drawn out. Thoughts of listening can bring on memories of sitting through long, drawn-out meetings or being cornered by someone telling a long story that only they care about. Actually, there is no listening going on in these situations. We are a conscripted audience whose good manners prevent us from jumping up and walking away.

Dynamic Listening is an active sport. It takes practice, focus and creativity. Dynamic Listening is the fundamental play for building relationships and getting what you want. It brings real information out in the open to actually solve problems and innovate new solutions. Instead of emotions confusing the issue, Dynamic Listening organizes the facts and feelings into a driving force that is headed in the right direction.

Listening may be boring, but as a journalist friend told me years ago, Dynamic Listening is the most fun you can have with your clothes on. It is amazing what people will tell you if given a chance.

BASIC SKILLS

Dynamic Listening is the can opener that gets people talking at a deeper level than the surface. It is complete communication. Full communication requires two discussions. One half of the discussion is about the facts and content, the other half is about the energy...or emotions and feelings. Most of us have a preference. We either talk more about facts or talk more about the energy. Facts are more comfortable for some people because they believe facts are irrefutable. People perceive there is a right or wrong when it comes to facts and, with careful preparation, a person can always be right. Conversations based on facts appear to be objective with little chance of argument and conflict.

Other people are focused on harmony between people and prefer talking about feelings. Energy-based conversations assume the facts are obvious and strive to keep everyone engaged and happy. With this either/or of some conversations being about the facts and others being about engagement

between people, the question jumps out, So, why can't we do both? We need the facts AND the engagement!

One of my mentors during my doctoral program was a professor in Counseling Psychology. He had years of experience working with school counselors and groups of teachers in the school system. He found my perspective fascinating because I had a blind spot when it came to people's emotions – my focus had always been on the facts. I was clearly an oddity in my counseling courses with my focus on how things work.

I decided to put my newfound way of thinking about the people side into practice. I arranged to teach basic communication skills to senior engineering students, and my professor helped design the training. We also tried it out at a local engineering design company so he could help me grow in my new field. I'll never forget his observation after watching me and my technical audience wrestle with learning to communicate using both emotions and facts.

DR. BILL'S STORY OF
FACTS VS RELATIONSHIPS
I've worked with teachers my whole career, particularly in elementary schools. We would get a project funded and go to work. By the end of our second meeting, everyone knew everyone else in the room, about their children, and where they lived. It was fun to meet and the conversations were great. If someone had a problem attending, the

group was understanding. However, after about six months, little real work had happened and things fell apart. I saw it over and over. They became great friends, but we didn't get the project done.

Then, in talking with these engineers, there are people who have worked together for a long time and they don't really know anything about many of the other people in the office. In our role plays, we can't even get them to say things like *You seem happy today* in an attempt to talk about the energy. They jump right in discussing the facts of the problem, but they can't seem to engage beyond the facts. In talking to them, I've learned that they become angry when people don't let them know when they aren't coming to meetings and when they believe no one is listening to them. Then, because of the bad relationships, the project falls apart. It might get done, but it is not as successful as it could have been. There are too many negative feelings. And, they don't really want to work together again from the misunderstandings.

It seems the teachers are focused on the relationships and harmony, and the engineers are focused on the facts and content. Either way, things fall apart and the final project is not what could be. I never understood why we couldn't get great work from the teachers until I saw the engineering project fall apart because of a lack of relationships. With the teachers, we were missing the focus on the facts. It takes both a focus on the task and a focus on the energy.

THE FACTS

Facts are boring. The facts are the numbers, specifications, calculations, budgets, and schedules. Without any energy applied, facts have no drive...no rock and roll. There is not one thing about a fact by itself that makes people want to get up and dance.

To get motion from facts, you must apply energy. I hear arguments from my students that some facts are so important, so persuasive...and certainly are not boring. However, facts only take on life when people apply their own personal values and beliefs.

Facts are important. They provide a basis for how things work so we can make good decisions. Facts provide details so we can coordinate with each other. However, agreeing on the facts isn't always easy. When we truly agree on the facts, then both the actual content and our feelings about the content's value are a match. In theory, it is impossible to disagree on facts because a fact is clearly defined. However, we disagree on the facts every day. The disagreement comes when we apply our own values and beliefs to the facts. We disagree on how the fact is used, how it was decided, and what it means. The disagreement is not on the fact itself – that can be resolved. The trouble comes with what it means, and what it means is different to each person based on their individual viewpoint. However, we rarely separate the actual fact from the fact as seen through our perspective.

A key skill is learning to speculate on the other person's perspective of the facts. Another way of saying this is *Consider what the facts might mean to the other person.* The goal is to interpret the other person's *why* about the fact. Interpreting the other person's *why* is most easily accomplished by putting yourself in their shoes by asking these questions:

- If what happened to them happened to me, what would I do or think? Maybe that is what is behind their actions.
- When that happens to me, here's what I do or think.
- If that was me, what would I be doing or thinking?

These questions can help you engage in problem solving about the meaning of your counterpart's actions.

THE ENERGY

The energy provides all the motion. Energy applied to facts makes things happen. Depending on the energy that is applied to the facts, different things happen. An example is when you ask someone to help you do something.

SUPERVISOR: John, I need for you to do your performance review input and get it to me right away. (Supervisor is thinking that John understands that he should stop whatever he is doing and prepare his performance review input.)
JOHN: I'll take care of it. (John is thinking that maybe after lunch he'll do it, but right now his favorite technician needs help getting a computer restarted. Plus, John believes that getting equipment to run is real work and performance reviews are busy work that always ends up being negative.)

This exchange is sure to create trouble. The supervisor doesn't consider that John probably doesn't value performance reviews, nor does the supervisor inquire about what John is doing so that priorities are established.

A better exchange that addresses the task and the energy to get it done would be:

SUPERVISOR: John, I need for you to do your performance review input and get it to me right away. I am guessing that you have other things you believe are more important, but in this case, I need for you to stop and spend an hour preparing your input. (The supervisor speculates on what actions John will be taking and then discusses them.)

Experts at describing the energy have a large vocabulary of words to tease out what is happening. Most of us have a total vocabulary of about 200 words. Frankly, we have a limited set of words to describe energy with only a handful of the 200 words devoted to feelings. We use a few words over and over at a general level of describing emotions. For instance, when we sense someone is happy, we might comment, *You seem happy, excited or great*; and when someone seems upset, we say, *You seem annoyed, mad, or angry*. When you can tease out emotional intensity by having more words that describe energy, then your communication will become clearer. For instance, when someone seems upset, you can choose the word that most accurately describes their feelings from a range of words describing angry. That range goes from barely angry to really angry (Annoyed...fed up...put out...furious...irate).

The first step in learning to talk about energy is to learn a vocabulary of words that suggest the range of emotional intensity. Expanding your range of words to describe emotions and feelings is the same as using the kindergarten box of eight crayons to color the world versus using the big set of over 100 crayons. You can get by with just a few words, but having more descriptors provides more accurate dialogue.

	Low		Medium		High
Happy	satisfied	cheerful	optimistic	thrilled	ecstatic
Sad	blue	uneasy	down	hurt	miserable
Angry	annoyed	fed up	put out	furious	irate
Confused	uncertain	disorganized	puzzled	upset	frustrated
Scared	cautious	edgy	nervous	threatened	intimidated
Weak	unsure	distracted	overwhelmed	embarrassed	inadequate
Strong	secure	determined	capable	powerful	aggressive

ENERGY WORD INTENSITY TABLE

A simple technique to help with finding the words to describe the energy and emotions is to describe yourself.

- When I am behaving in that way, I am [*insert descriptor from the Energy Word Intensity Table*].
- If I was [*that person*], and I texted my best friend about what was happening to me, I'd text...I am [*insert descriptor from the Energy Word Intensity Table*].
- The *What would I text*? question is my personal favorite because we are informal with our texts and often exaggerate to get the emotion of our message across in words. It's an easy way to come up with a word to describe feelings.

COMMUNICATING THE WHOLE PICTURE

Communicating the whole picture means that you describe the energy and the interpretation of what is happening about a topic. This technique can be difficult for those people with a preference for fact-based communication, because they are not comfortable speculating...especially about how someone feels! Complete communication requires guessing a feeling and guessing about what the real meaning might be. For those who prefer talking about emotions, it can also be difficult to pay attention to details in order to interpret what is behind the emotion.

Dynamic Listening requires that you guess the other person's emotion and what the facts mean based on your own personal experience. It can make you feel vulnerable and out of control when you start using the technique. In actuality, people will respond with agreement or they will correct you. In fact, most people are delighted that you are willing to ask about emotions and interpretation instead of just assuming you know how it is. It makes life much easier to be checking in about what you see and sense instead of making assumptions and acting without any real basis.

One night in my graduate-level Counseling Fundamentals class, we learned a technique for reflecting the emotion and the facts to clarify communication. I couldn't believe it. After years of communication training classes where I couldn't figure out how to put people skills training into action in real life, I saw a formula for what to do and suddenly I understood. This was my first formula and it is simple. You can make it more complicated, but it doesn't seem to work any better. In fact, the more complicated you make it, the more confusing it can seem to the person receiving the communication.

The basic formula has two parts. The first part is to reflect what you believe the emotions to be. The second part is where you state your interpretation of what is happening.

You seem [*insert descriptor from the Energy Word Intensity Table*] because [*insert your interpretation about what is going on*].

Once you have the basic formula mastered, you can turn it into a can opener to get at all kinds of information by adding on a Door-opener. Door-openers are simple phrases that work with any situation. They don't presume any facts. The point of the Door-opener is to get the other person to tell you a story or example about what has happened.

SOME FAVORITE DOOR-OPENERS ARE:
- Tell me about the last time that happened
- Give me an example
- Tell me more
- Tell me what mattered the most

Please notice that these door-openers do not offer any suggestions or advice, they simply invite the other party to share more information.

EXAMPLES

A CONVERSATION BETWEEN JACK AND JEN
AT THE END OF A LONG DAY

JACK: Hey Jen, it's good to be home after a long day. How was your day?
JEN: I had a terrible day. I hate my job. I can't believe my boss.

Jack has a choice here. He can use Dynamic Listening to help Jen calm down, or he can fuel the misery.

JACK: (Healthy Response) You seem really upset about what happened at work today. It seems to me that things are getting worse at your job. Tell me about it.

JACK: (Unhealthy Response) I told you that job was trouble when you took it. I think you need to tell your boss to leave you alone.

A CONVERSATION BETWEEN JANET AND TRISH ABOUT THE BREAKUP OF A RELATIONSHIP

JANET: I can't believe my boyfriend dumped me today with a text.
TRISH: (Healthy Response) Oh Janet, I know getting dumped by text is upsetting because he didn't even have enough respect to let you know in person. You seem furious because he is acting like you didn't have an important relationship. Tell me more...
TRISH: (Unhealthy Response) He is such a jerk. Oh well, that's just how guys are these days.

A CONVERSATION BETWEEN CHARLIE AND PETER ABOUT A POTENTIAL EQUIPMENT PURCHASE

CHARLIE: OK team, we need to make a final decision on which controller to buy. I talked with John from IT and he says we should get the XYZ controller.
PETER: (Healthy Response) Charlie, you seem to have made up your mind about what we should purchase. We had some problems with that controller last year. How have you accommodated what we learned from the past experience?
PETER: (Unhealthy Response) Are you crazy! We were forced into that purchase last year by IT and it never has worked!

PAINTING THE ELEPHANT

In every conversation, whether it is with one person or many people, there is an invisible elephant in the room. This invisible elephant is what is unsaid and the opinions and assumptions that people brought with them to the conversation. This technique is designed to take the elephant from invisible, where everyone pretends it is not there, to visible so you can talk about it and agree on what is now there in plain sight.

Once you paint the elephant with an energy word and describe what you believe is happening, then the conversation can turn to working things out. Here's an example of *painting the elephant*. Imagine entering a meeting room, and the temperature feels cold as ice even though the thermostat on the wall says the room is a normal temperature.

Hello everyone. The temperature in this room feels cold as ice, and I don't mean the temperature on the thermostat. I am thinking that many of you are frustrated because we are going to be working overtime during the holiday break. Let's talk about how we choose to handle this unfortunate situation.

At this point, the people in the room don't need to act out their frustration because it has been acknowledged and there is an invitation to talk about it.

OPENING THE CAN

Dynamic Listening means you are listening to other people in a way that allows you to observe what is being said and then restating what you believe it meant, both emotionally and factually. When you ask for an example, it is like opening a can and information, both facts and emotions, will come bubbling out.

One of the best ways to really get to the facts is to engage people in a story about when something similar happened. For example, if you are talking about a change, telling a story of what the future will be can get them talking about their viewpoint. If you are problem solving, getting the people involved to tell the story about the last time the problem happened can provide information that never comes out in a fact-finding interrogation.

Dynamic Listening with the goal of facilitating people to talk about real life examples and stories provides emotional signals and information beyond the facts. Putting words on emotions and stating what is behind the facts gets people engaged. Then using a Door-opener opens the can. More information comes spilling out, and in a way that gets around assumptions and stereotypes.

WARNINGS ABOUT USING DYNAMIC LISTENING

Although using Dynamic Listening is not a dangerous activity, there are a few things you should know. I've heard these reports about its use consistently over the years.

- **WHAT DID YOU DO?** Is the accusation you might get from your Significant Other when you start using this technique at home. If your usual response is Hmmmm... or giving advice to solve their problem, your Significant Other will immediately sense that you are behaving differently and ask you about it. They will assume you are up to something. The best answer is to own up that you are indeed up to something and it is a better way to communicate. Admit that you are abandoning your bad habits, and would really like to hear the whole story.
- **DON'T YOU DR. PHIL ME!** People will notice if you suddenly start showing interest in their feelings after years of focusing on the facts. Again, the best answer is to own up that you learned a new way to communicate, you are abandoning your bad habits, and would really like to hear what is going on.
- **MY FAVORITE WARNING** Is that this technique changes the conversation. People like to be seen. When you hold up a mirror for them by talking about who they really are and how they feel, connections happen. Once you put labels of energy words on emotions and describe what you believe has happened, people open up to relationships and share information. You build trust. Be prepared to learn more from your family, co-workers, and those around you than you dreamed possible. When you start using Dynamic Listening, get ready for Extraordinary Performance.

PLAY #3
CURIOSITY AND THE ART OF POSITIVITY

My formal education has been in colleges of Engineering, Education, and Business. I have been a teacher or student in engineering, sport psychology, counseling psychology, management, and MBA programs. Each discipline has taught me a different way of thinking about accomplishing tasks and building relationships. There have been a few perspectives that I didn't believe at first. However, as time has passed, I've come to understand that they all contribute to creating Extraordinary Performance.

One morning in my graduate-level Sport Psychology class, another student was talking about how an athlete was acting out – seemingly playing in a self-centered way and not being much of a team player. We were all sports fanatics and most of us had a low opinion of this talented athlete who appeared to be focused on playing for the limelight. After listening to our argument for a few minutes, the professor interjected and used this real life example from sport for a teaching moment I have never forgotten.

HE'S JUST DOING THE BEST HE KNOWS HOW TO DO.

We argued back with examples of how not being a team player was costing games. Our professor said, "I didn't say he was doing the right thing or even a good thing. I just said he is doing the best he knows how to do. Our job in sport psychology is to figure out why he thinks his actions are winning behaviors and then help him get on track with the team."

I pondered this viewpoint for several months. I couldn't see how behaviors that were clearly wrong should be given any credence. Finally, I understood, and I have a conversation with almost every person I coach about *how people are doing the best they know how to do.* Not the best thing, sometimes not even a good thing, but in that person's eyes, they are doing the best they know how to do. I finally understood that having a Curiosity about what was going on instead of evaluating right and wrong was the key to actually solving problems and creating extraordinary outcomes. *Curiosity* replaces *Evaluation* in the Extraordinary Life.

I'M DOING MY BEST

This play becomes extremely hard to understand when the 8% that have some other motivation on their mind are part of the group. Those people in the 8% have no intention of working with everyone for success, so I encourage you to forget about them for this play until you have it at an expert level. Even if you are an expert at helping people perform, remember that the 8% may be so focused on their own personal motives that they won't consider change.

Once we cut out the 8%, we are left with the 92%. This is the rest of the group and they came to work hard to achieve remarkable performance and lives. They welcome ideas about improving and have an attitude of positivity when encouraged. Here's how Curiosity works in place of evaluation to create Extraordinary Performance.

SUPERVISOR'S OBSERVATION: Wow, look at what Mark is doing. I can't believe that he is making so many mistakes in recording the results.
RESPONSE 1 – EVALUATIVE SUPERVISOR: Mark, you are not doing your job correctly. You must not have been paying attention during training. I don't know if you are smart enough for this task. I need for you to do this job to specs. If you can't do the job correctly, I'll be forced to write you up.
RESPONSE 2 – CURIOUS SUPERVISOR: Mark, I know we trained you and you did well on the proficiency performance test. I am watching you and it looks to me like there are lots of mistakes with the results you are recording. I can't make sense of what is happening between your performance on the training and how you are now doing the job. Can you explain to me what's going on so we can work it out?

Needless to say, these two different responses to Mark's behavior will get the supervisor very different reactions from Mark. In response 1, the supervisor has taken on an evaluative perspective where Mark is being evaluated and comes up short. The supervisor sees no reason that Mark should be making mistakes because he has passed the training program.

In response 2, the supervisor has started with the perspective that Mark is *doing the best he knows how to do* even though his outcomes are not correct. The supervisor is checking out what is going on by not assuming the source of the mistakes. The supervisor is curious and anxious to explore if the problem is in interpretation of the recording of results, knowledge of expectations, or any other misunderstanding. This supervisor doesn't have to be angry.

Instead, the attitude is Curiosity about what is happening. Curiosity creates an atmosphere of exploration rather than one of negativity and punitive actions.

Having an attitude of Curiosity does not mean you ignore bad behavior or problems. It means instead of jumping to a conclusion about what has happened, you simply decide that something unexpected has happened and deserves exploring. You become extremely curious about what is going on.

When people are experts at a process or skill, it is easy for them to jump to a solution. Their experience allows a recognition of cues no one else may notice and they quickly grasp what is going on. Unfortunately, this quick jump to action and decision is not always correct. Even when they are correct, others can feel as if they didn't have a voice or all the information wasn't revealed. This type of behavior can cause people to believe that their input isn't valued, with a resulting attitude of compliance or *I'll do whatever you say. No more and no less. You didn't want my input, so even if I see something wrong, I'll just do my job the way you told me to.*

I coach people with years of experience and expertise to convert all of their knowledge to Inside Information. I encourage them to bring along those who are younger or less experienced by using their insights to ask good questions. The script for using inside information to be curious is:

EXPERT: It seems we have a problem here. I worked with this type of process before and from that experience, I know [*talk about what you know*]. I am looking at what happened and it seems that something else is going on that I can't understand. Could one of you help make sense of this for me?

At this point, others are invited to tell their side of the story of what has happened and why. In the process of learning what all sides believe and understand, a better picture of the real root cause of the problem will emerge.

When it comes to solving problems, it seems quick and easy to just size up the situation, tell others what to do, and move on to the next problem. However, this technique doesn't work for two reasons.

First, in the midst of all the repeating problems that probably deserve a simple *Do This* response, there are a few problems that look like the same old problems, but are actually something different. In fact, as humans we work hard to make problems match-up with ones we have already solved. Thus, bad decisions are easy to make when we don't take the time to do any exploration to verify that we truly had the correct solution.

Second, even if you know the correct next steps and the solution, it doesn't bring the rest of the team along when the conversation is evaluative.

The exploration from Curiosity addresses both the facts of the problem and how people came to arrive at their actions. It creates buy-in while educating about how to recognize the cues of the scenario so the problem doesn't keep happening.

CURIOSITY AND POSITIVITY

Someone who is curious comes across as interested and open. Positivity depends on openness to new ideas and dialogue about what is happening. It provides an opportunity for everyone to participate. Being curious and asking questions based on your experience and assumptions is not meant to be manipulative or to make others seem stupid. It is exploring.

Using *Curiosity* as part of a practice of Positivity requires a genuine interest in what has happened. If you know what has broken, be curious about what caused it to break. If you see an incorrect answer, be curious about how a wrong result could have been determined to be correct.

If you have a habit of being right and letting everyone know you are right, here is a helpful game to use to shift your thinking from being evaluative to being curious.

STEP 1: DECIDE THAT WHATEVER YOU THINK IS WRONG. This thinking will force your brain to abandon your old perspective because second-guessing doesn't make sense to evaluative thinking. For instance, if you know that there are always three crews working on Mondays and you see five, decide that somehow you must have had wrong information and set about discovering how you might have misinterpreted the scenario.

STEP 2: BELIEVE THAT EVERYONE IS DOING THEIR BEST. Recognize that everyone came to do good work, so there must have been some sort of misunderstanding. Your role is to take what you know and check it out with other people to discover the misunderstanding.

The words *discover* and *explore* are the action words for being curious. Once you abandon evaluation in favor of curiosity, you'll become incredibly amazed at what you discover. You'll find that much of the time no one had the entire story. In the process of facilitating everyone to share what they know and what they expected, you'll uncover new information that creates the attitude of positivity that is the basis of Extraordinary Performance.

PLAY #4
GIVING ADVICE

ELAINE'S 1ST LAW OF COMMUNICATION
You can give all of the advice you want, but people rarely take it. You are just wasting your time and breath because most people can't hear advice. I didn't say your advice isn't good, I'm just telling you that people generally don't take advice.

Giving Advice is a communication habit that tears down relationships one helpful suggestion at a time. Giving Advice is telling your opinion to someone else about what they should do. It is fixing the other person's problem without a dialogue about the root cause. Giving Advice shuts down conversation. It is a form of criticism, because although it is delivered as a kind suggestion, it is actually a correction. Giving Advice is veiled criticism, and criticism is one of John Gottman's relationship killers. Even when people ask for advice, it is unwise to believe the communication between the giver and receiver is accurate without clarification from both parties.

Giving Advice and education are different. Education is teaching someone what to do. Education starts with a dialogue to discover the problem. Then the second step is uncovering possible solutions, and concluding with a game plan for how to put a solution into play. Giving Advice happens in seconds with a quick delivery such as *Why don't you...* and education takes minutes and hours to develop real understanding so that change can happen.

The reason people don't take advice and are actually offended by helpful suggestions is because without a dialogue to discover the actual problem, the well-intentioned advice comes across in a way that makes the other side push back or stonewall. When the advice is based on a misunderstanding of the real problem, the receiver often becomes defensive and the advice giver more insistent. It creates a negative vibe.

KATLYN: Parking is terrible every morning! I have to park about a mile from here just to get a spot and then walking in is another 15 minutes. I can barely get here on time.

MANDY: If you would get here at 7:15 instead of 8:00, you could get a closer place. There are plenty of close parking spots available at 7:15. (This statement is advice that implies the problem is because Katlyn is running late.)

KATLYN: (now in defensive mode) Well, I can't get here any earlier because I have to drop my child off at daycare and don't want to force her to get up any earlier. I'd rather inconvenience myself instead of my baby. (This simple exchange of advice giving has set a tone of negativity for these two people.)
MANDY: (sensing the tension in Katlyn's voice) You don't have to be so testy. I was just trying to help.

Giving Advice is hard work. It is the opposite of Dynamic Listening™. Dynamic Listening follows a script of reflecting what you see and hear and then interpreting the meaning. It inquires about emotions and events. Giving Advice assumes meanings and provides answers based on those assumptions. Without the preliminary exploration of Dynamic Listening, Giving Advice frequently feels like being poked by the advice giver instead of being offered a helping hand.

If your habit is bouncing in and fixing things with advice, Dynamic Listening can seem like a lot more work because it takes some thinking to consider the emotions and what has happened beyond your assumptions. However, Giving Advice stirs up unwanted emotions and damages relationships. There are four options when you feel the urge to Give Advice.

Option 1 is to actually Give Advice and be prepared for the fallout from creating negativity and then having to do repair work. Option 2 is to do nothing. Doing nothing means that you keep your intended good advice to yourself. While you might not build a connection, you don't damage the relationship either. Option 3 is acknowledging the other person's difficulty by using Dynamic Listening to build a connection through Painting the Elephant (see the Dynamic Listening play for a description of this concept). Option 4 builds on Dynamic Listening to engage in problem solving to help the other person.

KATLYN: Parking is terrible every morning! I have to park about a mile from here just to get a spot and then walking in is another 15 minutes. I can barely get here on time.
MANDY: You seem frustrated because parking so far away puts you in a rush and almost makes you late every morning. (Option 3 – Dynamic Listening response. The elephant in the room of almost being late and having such a long walk is put together in a meaningful summary along with addressing Katlyn's emotion.)

Giving Advice is a damaging habit. Breaking yourself of this habit has two components. The first is stopping yourself from Giving Advice, and the second is learning how to give your valuable advice in a way that other people can hear it and act on it.

STOPPING GIVING ADVICE

When I teach this topic in my classroom, my students are pushing back by this point in the lecture. They say *my friends…we give each other advice all the time. It's no big deal. We like it.* My counterpoint is to ask them to spend the next week not giving advice and observing what happens between people when the advice giving starts. A few weeks later, I ask the class to tell me what they have decided about Giving Advice. Their responses sound like this:

My roommate is always complaining about her boyfriend. I used to tell her what to do, thinking I was being helpful. It seemed the same conversation happened over and over. She never changed anything. Then I tried what we learned in class and said, *You seem hurt because your boyfriend says he is going to meet you and then doesn't show up* instead of *You need to dump that jerk. He doesn't respect you.* When I let her talk, she decided what to do and has made changes. It is a lot easier to just listen and help her understand what she is saying. Plus, she didn't get mad at me.

My students in the workplace tell the same story, except about what happens among people at work. My adult students frequently use Option 2 because they have recognized their advice is actually their personal opinion. They understand that not Giving Advice means you stay within your personal boundaries by being respectful and not assuming that how it is for you is how it is for the other person.

It is actually easy to stop Giving Advice. It is a two-step process where the first step is to catch yourself about to Give Advice, and the second step is to keep your mouth shut.

STEP 1: The first step is to recognize that you are *fixin' to* Give Advice and just stop. Fortunately, most of us use key phrases to deliver our advice. Advice giving usually starts with one of these key phrases:

WHY DON'T YOU...
YOU NEED TO...; YOU DON'T NEED TO...
YOU SHOULD...; YOU SHOULDN'T...
YOU COULD...; YOU COULDN'T...

To stop Giving Advice, you use your self-coach discussed in the chapter on How-To Change. Your self-coach has limited capability, and is most functional when used to alert you that a signal has happened. You program your self-coach to send a STOP whenever you start to use one of these key phrases of Giving Advice. From my personal experience, you'll get about half of one of these phrases out and then stop in mid-sentence. You'll realize that you are about to deliver advice and then mumble about forgetting what it was you planned to say.

STEP 2: The second step is to actively decide which option is best for this situation. Most of the time you will simply use Dynamic Listening to acknowledge the other person or say nothing. Saying nothing can be its own trap as people may feel ignored. However, once you get stopped from delivering a negative statement, you can consider your options.

GIVING ADVICE THAT CAN BE HEARD

Most of us have good advice for other people. We observe them interacting with others and have inside information about what is happening. We want to share our own experiences that have created success. Giving Advice is a wonderful way to connect when you understand three basic fundamentals and use a script based on educating instead of telling. Giving Advice that can be heard uses a coaching model based on helping people understand the problem and what to do to improve.

THE FUNDAMENTALS

You can talk for hours, but the other person must be in a frame of mind to hear you. Three fundamental concepts that make advice more readily heard are:

BANKRUPTCY – The recipient of the advice is more likely to hear you when they believe improvement is necessary and they have no other options. They are bankrupt. Sometimes, as in the case of the Skeet Shooter in the How-To Change chapter, the recipient has their own ideas and will go and try these first. When they discover that they really have no better options, they become willing to try the advice. It is usually worth the time and effort to explore their ideas and debunk the bad ones to establish bankruptcy. If the other side is basing their plan on bad information and incorrect perceptions, establishing bankruptcy is crucial for opening them up. You will need to reflect their emotions and what you think their beliefs are to move into the discussion zone.

DISOWN YOUR ADVICE – It is important to make sure the advice is not perceived as your opinion or a plan that is unique to you. Disowning the advice means that you preface ideas with *Would you like to hear some ideas?* instead of *Let me tell you what I did*. Sometimes I have pushback from people who believe it is dishonest to not let the other side know of their own personal solution. However, attaching the idea to you or another specific person can provide excuses about changing. The recipient can fall back on *But I am not like [you/someone else] and that's why it won't work*. Also, recipients often are reluctant to be open when ideas don't work out because they don't want to disappoint you. They feel their performance is being compared to yours and wasn't successful. Comparison to others is difficult feedback to swallow, and it is important to keep comparison out of coaching. Comparison is only useful in helping people when it is comparison to standards – not other people.

GIVE CHOICES – When you insist on coming up with alternatives and choices, it forces the other side to open up to more than their current viewpoint. Even when the person receiving the advice comes up with your preferred option first, insisting on finding other options signals the subconscious that this isn't the one and only solution. It lets the other person know change may take a few iterations. Once the other person starts generating options, the conversation becomes positive with a focus on how to improve.

Generating other options helps finalize the chosen plan through a discussion of pros and cons for putting their choice into action.

THE FORMULA FOR GIVING ADVICE

Giving Advice that can be heard is a 5-step process. It takes time and patience. It's wise to start with an agreement from the other party that they would like to come up with some ideas and an action plan for improving their situation.

Your goal is for the recipient of the advice to have a clear understanding of the problem and an action plan of steps at the conclusion of the conversation.

STEP 1: ARTICULATE THE PROBLEM. The recipient of the advice must state the problem. Until you hear them say it out loud, it is unclear what they are working on. It is easy for the educator to see the problem and describe it. But until the person with the problem can state it clearly and provide an example of when it happens, it is a waste of time to move on. If the two sides are describing two different problems, yet think they are talking about the same thing, it leads to hard feelings. Sometimes the hardest part of the conversation is reaching an agreement on the real problem.

STEP 2: GENERATE CHOICES. The first tip is to either get their ideas on the table or establish bankruptcy. It is crucial that you do not tell your thoughts first. Most likely, you'll hear them say that they have no ideas, but you can use teasers such as *If you could do anything, what would it be? What have you seen other people do?*

Once you state your ideas, they will most likely shut down their own thinking and latch onto one of your suggestions. If you make the mistake of putting out a suggestion by saying that it is what you would do, then you have claimed ownership and it will be more difficult to have open conversations and develop an action plan they will use.

Your objective is to get their ideas out on the table first, your ideas second, and then to be what we call an honest broker. An honest broker insists on discussing both the good and bad points. An honest broker doesn't overlook problems, but instead encourages the other side to face up to them.

STEP 3: CHOOSE AN IDEA AND DEVELOP AN ACTION PLAN. Once you get several ideas developed so that there are choices, it's time to work with the advice recipient to pick their favorite idea and start to generate the steps to put it into motion. Again, your job is to be an honest broker to help them understand what makes sense.

After they pick an idea and can speak it back to you so you know that both of you are thinking the same thing, it's time to develop an action plan of steps to put the plan into action. Each step needs a definite action and a schedule, then they will put it into practice.

STEP 4: GET COMMITMENT TO THE FIRST STEP. Once you have the action plan, your objective is to encourage the other party to commit to the first step toward improvement. Again, they must state their action and when they will have it done, or you should consider this just a conversation of speculation.

STEP 5: CHECK IN AND CONFIRM. If you are a real friend, then mark on your calendar the action plan steps and when they agree to do them. Then, after their start date, check in to see how it went. A great perspective is to assume that they took action, and you simply ask, "I recall you were going to do [*state their action*] by [*state their date of the action*]. It's after that date. How did that go for you?"

If they did not take the action, your next statement is, "So, it is still a great action. When do you think you can do it now?" And, as you can guess, you check in with them again after that date. If they took action, you ask them, "So, remind me of the next step and when you plan to do it. What are you thinking about the next step?"

At this point, you are probably thinking to yourself *Who has time to go through all of those steps to just pass along information?* The point of improving how you *Give Advice* is to understand the commitment it takes to help people change and learn new behaviors. The quick tip doesn't confirm that both parties are talking about the same problem. Once you truly understand the process, you'll find that just saying nothing is usually the best option when you feel the urge to quickly solve someone else's problem.

However, this structured coaching program for Giving Advice isn't always so tedious. As a faculty member with an expertise in performance, I am often asked by my undergraduates about how to study better. Here's how that conversation usually goes, with notes about how I do it using the 5-Step technique.

STUDENT: Hi Dr. Seat. I am doing terrible this semester. Can you help me?
ELAINE: (Step 1) So, tell me what do you mean you are doing terrible?

STUDENT: Well, my grades are about average, and I really want them to be a 3.0 or better.

ELAINE: (Step 2) What are you thinking would help you?

STUDENT: (Notice the Faulty Thinking) I am thinking I should just study harder. Focus more.

ELAINE: So, when you say study harder, you are thinking of doing more of what is already not working? And by focus more, what will you need to do to increase focus? I am thinking you are describing outcomes instead of actions to achieve those outcomes.

ELAINE: (Step 2, establish bankruptcy) What ideas do you have about what you can do?

STUDENT: Well, I don't really have any ideas.

ELAINE: (Step 2, disown the ideas) I've worked with a lot of students. Would you like to hear some things that seem to work for them?

At this point, I discuss three or four techniques that help students learn. It is important to not put the solutions out there in a way that worked for me. With my undergraduates, they say *But you are smart. You have a PhD. Why should I expect that to work for me?*

ELAINE: (Step 3) We've talked about several ideas. Which one do you believe would work to help you learn and perform better in school?

STUDENT: I think that finding a set place on the quiet floor of the library where I can always go to do work, and then going there instead of just hanging out would be a great idea.

ELAINE: (Step 4) So, what is the first step and when can you do it?

STUDENT: Well, I guess I just need to walk over to the library during my breaks when they are longer than 30 minutes. I guess I could start next week.

ELAINE: It's Monday now. When is your next break longer than 30 minutes so you can get started?

STUDENT: Well, I have a break in the morning, Tuesday, for two hours from 9-11a.m. I guess I could go then.

ELAINE: Sounds great. Good luck with this plan. I am confident it will help you.

ELAINE: (Step 5, on Wednesday night in class, speaking privately to the student) I remember that yesterday was when you were going to start using the library to study. How did that go?

STUDENT: Oh, I didn't make it. I just hung out in the coffee shop.
ELAINE: No problem. What held you back…When are you going to get started? How about tomorrow?

And the cycle continues…

Once you stop Giving Advice when people bring up a problem and instead reflect back to them how you believe they feel and why, you'll find that people are drawn to you. We like to be understood, and it's rare that someone sees our emotion and reflects it back. Replacing the advice giving with a positive habit creates a huge swing in how you interact with others. It makes you more open and promotes the freedom to discuss both creative and difficult topics. This freedom of exchanging information is a key component of creating Extraordinary Performance.

PLAY #5

FYI: FI'S VS. FD'S

If your discipline requires a heavy helping of mathematics, accounting, finance, or the physical sciences, you are what I call a Counter. If your passion is finding and manipulating patterns in art and music – you are also likely to be good at counting.

When it comes to working with people, Counters are most likely in trouble. Counters and friends of Counters might be offended by this statement and accuse me of using stereotypes to put people in boxes, but I'm just the messenger passing along the results of the research. The good news is that the difficulties that go along with being a Counter are specific. So help is on the way with specific strategies to guide improvements for the Counters. If you work or live with Counters, this information can help you understand them and make life easier.

Whether you are a Counter or a friend of a Counter, the purpose of this play is to help you understand your gift when it comes to taking in information and deciding what to do with it. Getting to the actual play will take some development, so gather up a dose of patience. First, I need to explain what the researchers found, and then I'll make sense of the findings and provide the specifics for several plays.

THE RESEARCH

Researchers Herman Witkin & Donald Goodenough spent their careers studying cognitive style, or how people take in and assemble information. Cognitive style is not a trait you are born with and are stuck with for life. It's about how you think and learn and can be altered with diligent practice. Witkin & Goodenough's terminology for cognitive style was Field Independence and Field Dependence. In their research, the field is the surrounding environment, and independence and dependence refers to how much attention a person gives to their surroundings in solving problems and making decisions.

Field Independence (FI) and Field Dependence (FD) are perhaps best understood by explaining the two tests used to determine FI/FD. The first test uses a rod and frame apparatus. This rod and frame test rig is basically a picture frame that is mounted on the diagonal and a straight rod that is mounted inside the frame. The frame and the rod can be rotated independently of each other. It would be like looking at a picture hanging on the wall that is not level, but in this case, it is hanging with the four corners of the frame hanging like a diamond shape.

To conduct this test, the subject is placed in a dark room for 15 minutes sitting in front of the rod and frame rig. The person loses their visual spatial orientation after this amount of time in the dark. Fundamentally, the subject loses all sense of up and down because of the lack of a visual reference. Then the frame in the test rig lights up where the person is looking at a rectangular shape (the outside frame) that is rotated off center (by off-center, the points of the frame are not in vertical alignment). The person is then asked to line up an inner rod to vertical by turning a handle that rotates the rod. Field dependent people are influenced by the frame and tend to line the rod up with the sides of the frame, while field independent people ignore the frame and line the rod up close to vertical.

The second test also measures how an individual is influenced by their surroundings. In this test, the subject is placed in a room that has walls, a floor, a roof and a ceiling. In the front wall there is a door and two windows. The entire room sits on a rotating pivot point (gimbal) with side-to-side rotation so that it can be rotated to a slant just like the frame. A chair is placed in the center of the room, facing the door, and it rotates independently of the room. Imagine the room is the frame, and the person sitting inside the room on the chair is the rod. The room will slant toward one side and then the person can rotate their chair to a different angle.

In the test, the subject sits on the chair in the room and the lights are turned off for 15 minutes. While the lights are off, the room is slowly rotated to a slant. Then the lights are turned back on and the subject is asked to rotate their chair so that they are vertical. Field Independent people tend to shut

FIELD INDEPENDENT   FIELD DEPENDENT

their eyes and sense vertical with their bodies. They rotate their chair until they are sitting in a way that feels straight up and down. Field Dependent people say to themselves *Well, door frames are straight* so they rotate to line themselves up with the door frame.

These two tests demonstrate the effect that the environment has on these two cognitive styles. When they close their eyes to shut out the room to sense vertical, FI people are using information that is independent of the surroundings. They make their decision internally and what is going on around them is ignored. The other group (FD) checks out the surrounding room and aligns with the environment. They are basing their action on what is going on around them (FD).

Once Witkin & Goodenough determined that people had two different basic responses, they started exploring other characteristics that accompanied the two cognitive styles. For instance, FI people are more skilled at technical problem solving and pattern recognition, while FD people excel at interpersonal interactions. When it comes to learning, FI people are not affected by the room and environment. They are at their best when left alone to figure out and internalize the pattern. FD people need a more structured learning environment and focus more on external cues such as the room, the instructor, and the dialogue. They want to talk about the material. FD people prefer learning material that is not formula and pattern-based unless it can be translated into a dialogue.

Witkin & Goodenough's studies attempted to understand the nature of scientists in an effort to create more technical prowess after World War II. For our purposes, their research provides insights about the positives and the negatives that go along with being FI or FD.

THE RESULTS: FIELD INDEPENDENCE & FIELD DEPENDENCE

Witkin & Goodenough's research is summed up in the table *Characteristics of Field Independent & Field Dependent Persons*. A quick explanation of each row by Characteristic sets the stage for several insights.

CHARACTERISTIC: INTERPRETS WORLD

The ability to dis-embed is the key factor that drives the other characteristics. However, it is a gift that comes with both good and bad outcomes. FI people have the ability to look at something, take it apart, and see the different pieces. They can look at the rod and frame and separate the rod from the frame to

Field Independent	Characteristic	Field Dependent
MD, engineer, computer scientist, scientist	Typical Occupations	Elementary school teacher, social worker, salesperson
Internal	Environmental focus	External
Dis-embeds into simple objects	Interprets world	Reflects what is observed
Weak	Interpersonal skills	Strong
Arrogant, aloof, manipulative, withdrawn, not caring, insensitive, dominant	Personality as experienced by others	Caring, sensitive to others needs, flexible, easygoing,
Withdraw, isolate	In conflict	Pursue to continue dialogue
Technological societies	Societal association	Agrarian societies
Scarcity	World view	Abundance

Characteristics of Field Independent & Field Dependent Persons

determine the best position to be vertical. In math classes, they were the ones who were good at word problems. They have the ability to look at a jumble of information, separate it into all components, and apply a set of rules and formulas to the reorganized pieces. They excel at dis-assembling, or dis-embedding, a complex system into its components so they can put it together in a different way for a new solution.

On the other hand, a word problem seems to be a senseless story to an FD person, and mathematics is a jumble. They have difficulty separating the problem into pieces. However, they can enter a room and determine how people in the room feel, and they readily negotiate with people because of their ability to pick up on the subtlety of human response. They can sell snake oil by picking up on phrases and non-verbals to guide the conversation.

LESSONS IN PERSPECTIVES: THE CAR SALESPERSON

I am Field Independent. I know this first because I have been successful in engineering school. My FI qualities are what drove me to understand getting along with people as a set of formulas and scripts. Although the following is not a true story, it would most certainly be how it would play out if I decided to be a car salesperson. I would be miserable and unsuccessful. If I were to sell cars, here's how the conversation would go when a Dad and his recently graduated high school daughter walked onto the car lot.

"Hey, congrats on graduating. Where are you going to college?" When they reply, "Oh, the University of Tennessee", I'd jump into full-blown FI problem solving mode and say, "Oh, parking is terrible and you won't have time to be tending to maintenance. Plus fancy cars are stolen all the time from the parking garages. Here's what you need...[*and I would point out a basic small car with a five-year full warranty*]. All you need to do is pick the color... red, white, black, blue...but don't pick red because you'll get more speeding tickets." At this point, the buyers would walk off and I would be mystified at what happened, because I would have solved their problem of choosing a car with my good advice.

However, a FD salesperson would handle it this way. "Hey, congrats on graduating. Where are you going to college?" When they replied, "Oh, the University of Tennessee", the conversation would proceed like this...

"Hey, that's great! I bet you can't wait to go to the football games! I have a couple of choices to start with. We have these convertible Miata's...you'd look really cool in one of these on campus...and then we have these great small cars that are easy to park and have a full maintenance plan so you can focus on school and we will take care of your car." If the Dad smiled at the thought of his daughter in a Miata, then the super salesperson would forget all about the more practical car. If the salesperson detected a frown at the convertible, and a sigh of relief about practicality, the super salesperson moves on to the small car with the warranty. It's all a matter of how you get your information and how you use it. I would be focused totally on their choice as a practical solution, and the successful salesperson would be picking up the cues about what the buyer wanted.

LESSONS IN PERSPECTIVES: THE BACHELOR PARTY

The following example of two men and their bachelor party illustrates just how differently people interpret a problem based on being FI or FD.

It is Thursday morning and Nathan is getting married on the upcoming Saturday. He and his best friend Jason are leaving for one last bachelor camping trip at their favorite spot – an island in the river at the foot of the mountains. Nathan flies out the next day at 1pm for the rehearsal dinner. The wedding is a big deal as his wife is from a large, well-known family and more than 300 guests have RSVP'd.

Getting to the airport is easy. The plane leaves at 1pm and it is about an hour's drive from the river to the airport. So, to check in at noon, the guys plan to be packed up and on the road at 11am.

Jason and Nathan have a great time fishing, camping, and reminiscing. However, during the night, a huge storm hits the mountains and the river changes from slowly drifting to flood stage with raging waters. Even though they are experienced canoeists, getting back to their Jeep from the island is tricky and dangerous.

What time should they leave the island, and how far upstream should they point the canoe to arrive back at their Jeep instead of way downstream in the lake?

FIELD INDEPENDENT   FIELD DEPENDENT

For the FI person, getting the boys to the airport on time is a math problem. Determining how fast the river is flowing and its width, along with the speed at which the boys can paddle is all that's needed to calculate their new route and timing. For the FD person, the focus jumps to the danger and the mess that will be created if Nathan misses his flight...or worse!

Solving problems requires that you first learn a framework or schema for the problem types. Then, when you see a problem, you first take it apart into all its pieces and make assumptions. This ability to mentally take something apart is called dis-embedding. Next, you decide the appropriate schema, proceed to fit the pieces you need and the best assumptions into the formula...and voila, out pops the answer. For instance, if a person has a degree in engineering, it is safe to assume that they are highly field independent – getting through engineering school requires the ability to dis-embed, recognize the schema, and then reassemble the pieces in a different manner to solve even the most basic first year engineering school problems. Success in disciplines that require high levels of problem solving are not simply a matter of trying. Along with persistence, it takes the dis-embedding skills of FI.

CHARACTERISTIC: OCCUPATION

FI people are the predominant cognitive style in occupations such as scientists, engineers, computer scientists, accountants, medical doctors, and professors. A solid assumption is that if a person has a degree in a field that requires a passing grade in advanced math such as calculus and advanced statistics, they are FI. Any field that requires taking information apart and rearranging it into different patterns at a high level most likely requires FI. Disciplines such as linguistics, art, and music are pattern based and also are hangouts of FI persons.

FD people migrate to jobs that focus on people. Social workers, super sales-persons, and elementary school teachers are clear examples. When the occupation depends on understanding the other person's perspective and building trust to make a personal connection, FD people excel. Some occupations require that personal connections be made almost immediately, and the FD style provides the ability to respond in the other person's voice. For instance, I have a dear friend who describes her gift as the ability to care-give for elderly persons. She has the patience to listen, and thrives on helping them with the simplest of tasks. At the University, she is a comfort to homesick freshmen. People immediately trust her, and she provides a safe space that helps them find solutions.

There are a few occupations that attract both cognitive styles. However, there is often misunderstanding when the person uses the opposite style from what is expected in the job requirements.

Pastors, ministers, and preachers are attracted to the ministry from both cognitive styles, which can result in problems. Here's what happens. Some Ministers focus on understanding and explaining the theology. This person studies and puts together a brilliant message each week attempting to influence the congregation with logic and interpretation of the passages in the original languages. Unfortunately, this FI minister who sees theology as a puzzle to be solved, typically isn't overly excited about tending to the flock with hand-holding, cheerleading, and arranging the Christmas Pageant. The congregation listens to the detailed sermons for about two years and then becomes disgruntled. They say *Our preacher really knows the Bible, but sure doesn't seem to care very much about us.*

Next thing you know, that pastor leaves and the church chooses a new preacher...one that smiles and seems to be in heaven on earth while bouncing babies and visiting the sick. All is well for a while. But this FD minister who chose ministry to provide a service to people, doesn't spend much time trying to put together and explain a puzzle for a sermon. You can guess what happens next. After a couple of years, the congregation begins to murmur *Our preacher is really good with the people and is a great friend, but we need more solid theology from the pulpit.*

So, a movement starts to send this pastor to another assignment and from a list of candidates, another FI pastor arrives to start the cycle again.

In another example, FD teachers migrate to the classrooms of young children. For pre-school and elementary school, the content is not difficult, so the ability to understand complicated topics in order to teach the material is not the issue. The difficulty is the connection with the youngsters, and FD teachers make this connection naturally while certainly being more than competent at the content. I learned this lesson from watching my friend Tara, a retired kindergarten teacher. Anywhere we went, young children ran to her. Tara has a big smile and bright dancing eyes. She had a knack for hugging kids and making them smile. I am a poster child for FI, and Tara is a perfect example of FD. I am also a college level teacher and would be a disaster as a kindergarten teacher. Tara has often said that she never wanted to teach kids any older than 4th grade.

Clearly, my friend Tara had the content of kindergarten mastered. The challenge of kindergarten teaching is to communicate with the young child when they might not have the words or developmentally reached that stage of being able to learn. Kindergarten teachers interpret how their young students perceive the world and figure out how to help them learn the basics of skills such as counting, the alphabet, and getting along in the group. It is more art than science, with every child being at a different place in their development.

Certainly, the best teachers at any level sense how to connect with the learner and explain the content. But as the content becomes more difficult, teachers focus on their task of delivery and evaluation instead of feelings and teaching social norms. Especially in the sciences and higher education, instructors are FI. Otherwise, they couldn't have made it through school themselves.

If I were a kindergarten teacher and one of my young students came up to me crying, I'd say, "What's wrong? You aren't bleeding...you seem warm/

cool enough…everything looks to be in order…so, stop crying and get back to what you are supposed to be doing." The crying would not stop. Parents would be storming the principal's office. Obviously I would not be successful as a kindergarten teacher. However, I can hear Tara's response to the same situation as she picked up on the cues. It would start with a hug and then she would say, "Oh honey, what happened? Are you OK? Here, let me see what's wrong…" After a moment the child would perk right up and skip away.

What I teach in the College of Business is complicated. My students don't expect a lot of compassion, and typically are just waiting to challenge an idea or the content. I push them to think more critically. For college instructors, class is never quite predictable because the questions and challenges by the students are not known in advance. As a FI teacher, I flourish in this world of analysis and on-the-spot putting together unique answers. Tara would be worn out by the details and would be focused on how the class felt at the end of the hour. Fortunately for us, our teaching positions have been a match to our cognitive styles.

This discussion of Occupations for the two styles often makes my students angry. People jump to the conclusion that since the occupations for FI people tend to be higher paying jobs, the implication is that being FI is better than being FD. This leap of insight is faulty.

Cognitive Style is not about smarts. It is about how we take in information and then process it. Tara and I both earned graduate degrees and successfully managed our careers and home life. We took in information and processed it differently. We were each better at different tasks due to FI/FD, but were equally successful.

Another faulty conclusion about FI/FD is based on a stereotype regarding intelligence. In our society, it is often presumed that excellence in math and science indicates intelligence. And, people working in occupations such as doctors, computer scientists, engineers, and scientists are presumed intelligent because of the difficulty of their education in the sciences. Actually, FI people are just better at math and science due to the way they can manipulate patterns, and many of those jobs often pay more. However, characteristics of FD people are an advantage in other jobs. FI/FD is not describing a degree of intelligence, but different types of intelligence.

CHARACTERISTIC: ENVIRONMENTAL INFLUENCE
FI people focus inward, often blocking out external cues and information they believe has no bearing on the situation. From being focused inward,

they don't notice what is going on around them. FD people focus on what is happening around them for information. They use the responses of others to guide their decision-making process.

FI people don't care about the facility, while the surroundings and tone greatly influences how FD people learn. FI people want to be left alone to study the topic so they can learn and internalize the structures, formulas, and patterns, while FD people want to discuss the topic and reach a conclusion with the group.

This characteristic has a tremendous influence on whether or not a person will be successful in their chosen career pursuit. If a person prefers solitary tasks such as reading and internalizing information, they thrive in programs that focus on patterns and problem-solving. On the other hand, if a person likes to figure things out through discussion and interaction, then topics such as math and science, where the textbook chapter concludes with pesky word problems, are going to be painful for them.

CHARACTERISTIC: INTERPERSONAL SKILLS

FI people were found to have weak interpersonal skills while FD people were found to have strong interpersonal skills. This characteristic is a result of FI people believing in their own analysis instead of relying on others to solve problems, while FD people have honed their interpersonal skills since they depend on others in problem solving. Having weak or strong interpersonal skills has nothing to do with being kind and caring. Interpersonal skills are referring to the ability to connect with other people.

Many years ago, I was on a business trip to San Jose, CA, before the internet and smartphones were available to provide information any where at any time. It was my first trip to the area and I arrived late in the afternoon. I asked the front desk clerk for the name of a nearby, decent place to eat and she suggested a famous Mexican restaurant. She told me to go to the foot of the hill, take a left and then at the building with the green roof, take a right and it would be on the right. If my cognitive style was FD, this would have been perfect information. But, I'm not and I needed to work it out step-by-step for myself. I thought it through and decided *What if I couldn't see the roof to find the turn in the dark!* I asked for the name of the restaurant, found the address in the phone book, took my map, and plotted the route because I need details and an internal plan.

CHARACTERISTIC: PERSONALITY AS PERCEIVED BY OTHERS

Witkin & Goodenough tested a group of people to determine whether they were FI or FD. Then the researchers asked other people who worked with each test subject to pick adjectives from a provided list that described the participant in the study.

The words chosen to describe the FI study participants were arrogant, aloof, manipulative, withdrawn, not caring, insensitive, and domineering. The words chosen to describe FD study participants were caring, sensitive to other's needs, flexible, and easygoing.

At this point, I generally have upset the FI people in my classes and they exclaim *But I'm not all those things. I'm a nice person and I care about people!* Notice that these findings did not measure how FI people meant to behave or how they felt about themselves and other people. The findings reported how other people experienced them, or the persona of FI and FD people as perceived by those around them.

Another study of FI/FD looking behavior helps explain what drives these perceptions. *Looking behavior* is how people look at others. The researchers found that FI people tend to NOT look at others who are talking to them, while FD people look directly at others while talking.

The explanation for these two different looking behaviors is that FI people just want the information and facts. They don't want the distraction of emotions and non-verbal signs. They don't want the story. They look away to better listen and absorb the information so they can then crank it through their schema and arrive at a conclusion.

FD people are connecting with the speaker to gather information and then interact about the subject. They prefer to make decisions with the help of their surroundings and dialogue with others.

I was embarrassed when I first read this research. It explained something about me! People would come to talk to me and stand in my office doorway. After a few minutes, the person would oddly look over their left shoulder to see who was standing there...except no one was ever there. This happened over and over.

FI people can have an off-putting habit when in conversation with someone. The habit is that of looking past the other person, looking away or looking down. The FI person does not make steady visual contact. This non-verbal sends a signal to the speaker that the FI person really does not want to talk with them or is not paying attention. No wonder people never came in and sat down. They didn't feel invited. As they stood in the doorway, I was looking past them at a spot over their left shoulder. That's why they kept turning around to see who was standing there! They thought I didn't care, when what I was really doing was giving them my full attention to the details of their words without being distracted by their non-verbals.

As fake as the solution sounds, I fixed my problem. I really don't like looking at people in the eye. I become distracted by what I see, and I think best when I can focus on listening and assimilating. My fix is to look at a spot just above their eyes. They get it that I am listening, and I start to pick up non-verbal signals that are also part of the data I need to ask better questions and use Dynamic Listening.

I have had to learn to do what caring, sensitive FD people do naturally.

CHARACTERISTIC: IN CONFLICT

Another characteristic of interpersonal skills that emerged from the research is that In Conflict, FI people tend to withdraw and isolate, while FD people want to pursue the issue and talk about it. These findings only make sense. The FI person wants to find a quiet spot to sort out the emotions and the facts to determine a solution. That action is their model of success. The FD person believes success comes from connecting and dialogue. They believe in sitting down, talking about the issue, and working it out. When FI and FD persons disagree, they are as likely to be angry about how they fight as to the actual topic of disagreement!

In conflict, the difference between the two cognitive styles causes the FI person to run away in an attempt to find the time to think, and the FD person chases them in an attempt to talk it out. The FI person feels threatened, the FD person feels ignored, and the conflict escalates.

CHARACTERISTIC: SOCIETAL ASSOCIATION

Witkin & Goodenough believed that being FI or FD was a result of our social upbringing's programming about what creates value. Their research found that there were more FI people in technological societies and more FD people in agrarian (farming) societies.

Technical societies place continual pressure to learn more science and facts. And, formal education rewards for those who perform best in school. It only makes sense that in the industrial world, this same pressure to perform with the highest rewards going to those who have demonstrated math-based ability creates a preferential status for individuals with FI characteristics. If you have the ability to problem solve, a technical society is set up to identify and nurture it.

In agrarian or farming-based societies, there is an emphasis on maintaining the community for the good of the group. The group, especially large families, pulls together to flourish in the good times and withstand the bad times. It takes the group to create the human labor to tackle big jobs, pull together to recover from natural disasters, and share resources. FD is encouraged and rewarded.

CHARACTERISTIC: VIEW OF THE WORLD

A characteristic that impacts how we think about success in extraordinary performing organizations is the worldview of FI and FD persons. This individual worldview is an outcome of the societal association. (The Introduction to the plays in the Math of Extraordinary section discusses the concept of worldview in more detail.)

The worldview of FI people is best expressed by a sense of scarcity, or there's only so much and when it's all gone, it will be used up. In a technical society, there seems to be universal truth that once all the natural resources are used up or all the jobs are filled, there will be no more. We believe the best decisions are data-based, which uses information from the past to predict the future. The emphasis is on learning to gather facts and putting those facts into schemas that guide accurate decision-making. The focus is not on the good of the group. It is survival of the fittest.

This worldview of scarcity or there is only so much and the amount is shrinking was evident in my engineering management career. I began my career at a nuclear weapons components manufacturing facility. Due to the end of the Cold War, the mission of my organization changed and we were faced with laying off technical professionals and staff. At the time, layoffs of professional staff were unheard of in this industry. People who worked at the facility expected to work hard, enjoy a good career, and eventually retire. Their mindset was to put down roots and be an integral part of the community for a lifetime. However, it was announced that layoffs were pending, and were necessary to align our staffing to match the new mission.

In technical organizations, the sense of scarcity is rampant. It is an unspoken mantra that originates from a predominance of FI employees. When pending layoffs were announced, individuals spent time calculating how much future work was funded in their specialty and justifying their individual job. There was no thought of taking all the work and splitting it up to keep everyone employed until more work could be identified and perhaps keep more people employed. There were arguments over keeping the best or keeping those with the most seniority. The cliché every man for himself, or the notion of scarcity, took hold with each person trying to protect their own job. Our office took on an air of secrecy as people retreated into themselves in true FI fashion.

The worldview of FD people is described as having a sense of abundance, or there will always be enough and even more. This attitude is reflected in agrarian societies where the good of all is the responsibility of the whole community. It is also reflected in the use of natural resources where even if there is a poor crop this year, there can be good weather and a bumper crop the next, supporting an attitude of abundance.

Flourishing is how FD people see the world. When you are your own prime resource, there is opportunity to do things differently and reap the rewards. Research in positive relationships has found that connecting with people creates energy. We become more energized when we spend time in positive connections. FD people thrive on connection and the energy created through interactions. They tap into the possibilities to move forward, and when engaging community with connection, they receive positive energy as a result.

THE PLAY

By now, you are wondering why the long explanation about FI/FD. The conclusions from this research are not kind to FI people when it comes to positive relationships. These plays are directed at helping FI people continue their problem-solving, while getting beyond their poorly perceived interpersonal skills. The goal is to provide methods and skills that allow their true spirit of cooperation and kindness to show, along with their ability to solve the most complex problems. Most FI people have a good heart and some not-so-good manners. These steps are intended to help improve the bad manners. If you are a FD person, this play can help you understand your FI friends, family and co-workers so you can smile at their idiosyncrasies instead of being aggravated with them.

STEP 1: REDEFINE WHAT YOU VALUE. FI people tend to value facts, and thus, ignore or dismiss emotions. An example of this thinking shows up in the poor looking behaviors. The starting place is a fundamental change in what you value. This change is usually a widening of what you believe is valuable information.

A life-changing way of thinking is to decide that how people are acting, their emotions, and their opinions are facts and information that impacts the schema and your ability to get the best decision or idea.

Use the formula in Dynamic Listening™ to pinpoint the emotion that will become facts. Considering the emotions and energy is half of the fact-finding process. The physical data is the other half of the information necessary for solving the problem.

STEP 2: MANAGE YOUR PRESENCE. Deliberately stop the behaviors that make you appear cold, aloof, manipulative, insensitive and all the other negative descriptors of how FI people are perceived. Let your true heart and spirit show through.

This step is incredibly important. I first read Witkin & Goodenough's research in 1994. It struck a chord and I immediately set about improving my bad manners. I didn't change my thinking process, but I changed how I went about engaging with people. I began physically looking at them in conversation. I baited myself into this behavior that felt awkward to me by deciding the emotions were valuable data that was also important in solving problems.

I quit behaviors that made me seem manipulative by joining the group rather than always focusing on the most efficient way to do things. My favorite example is a simple one that involves going to lunch. I was the one who always tried to figure out how to go in the least number of cars, find the least crowded times, or the best deal. I stopped being an efficiency expert and started enjoying the adventure.

The significance of my natural FI behaviors became even more apparent to me when in 2007, I read a study that seemed eerily familiar. The material was a table of *Characteristics that Derail Managers*. The first two items in the list were:

1. LACK OF SENSITIVITY TO OTHERS; ABRASIVE AND INTIMIDATING
2. ACTING COLD, ALOOF AND ARROGANT.

THE SAME WORDS USED TO DESCRIBE HOW PEOPLE PERCEIVE FI PERFORMERS

Seeing this same information from two different sources sparked my attention. It provided motivation for me to learn how to show my kind heart and flexibility. I knew staying with my current way of engaging with people was not an option. I could see where I had already paid a huge penalty for just being me with no filters. I had to fix my behaviors if I wanted to live an Extraordinary Life.

MATH OF THE EXTRAORDINARY™

INTRODUCTION TO THE RATIOS

PLAY #6
THE MAGIC RATIO

PLAY #7
WASTED NEGATIVES:
SARCASM AND CYNICISM

PLAY #8
DELIVERING THE ONE

PLAY #9
INQUIRY AND ADVOCACY

PLAY #10
THE RATIO OF CONNECTION:
OTHER VS. SELF

INTRODUCTION
THE RATIOS

In 2004, the results of a study by researchers Losada and Heaphy were published. These researchers were attempting to create predictive formulas that could "...run the nonlinear dynamics model that will portray what types of dynamics are possible for a [*organizational*] team." I haven't found much use for their model, and in fact, their statistics model that was used to create a predictive formula has been refuted.

However, the actual results of their experiment provide clear guidance for the communication plays that are the foundation of Extraordinary Performance.

THE EXPERIMENT

The actual experiment collected data from 60 companies by (1) observing the speech patterns of individuals during the work day and (2) determining a company performance rating. The companies ranged from small to large. Individuals were observed in activities of annual strategic planning, problem solving, and budget setting. Trained observers followed the individuals and carefully recorded their speech patterns as they engaged with others during their workday.

COMPANY PERFORMANCE RATINGS

Each company provided specific data for use in determining their company's performance score. The data included Profit and Loss statements, customer satisfaction data from interviews and surveys, and 360-survey data for the team members being observed. This data was plugged into a definition of performance that incorporated financials, customer feedback, and individual performance on interpersonal skills.

Based on the performance definition, a rating was assigned to each company as low-performing, medium-performing or high-performing. The financial data represented the company performance, the 360-survey data represented the individuals working at the company; and the customer feedback represented a combination of individuals and the company in the external marketplace. High performing teams had high marks in all three categories of submitted data. Low performing teams had low marks in all three categories. Medium performing groups were inconsistent in their scores with responses varying or in the middle.

COMMUNICATION RATIOS

Prior to the observations of interactions between people, the researchers selected types of speech communication patterns to be identified and tallied. Based on validated studies in communication and positivity, three proven speech behaviors in the form of a ratio of either/or were chosen for observation:

POSITIVE STATEMENTS TO NEGATIVE STATEMENTS. Positive statements provide support, encouragement, and appreciation; while negative statements suggest disapproval, sarcasm, and cynicism.

INQUIRY TO ADVOCACY STATEMENTS. Inquiry statements ask others what they think and encourage exploration of a topic. Advocacy statements tell what you think in an attempt to sell your viewpoint.

FOCUS ON OTHER VS FOCUS ON SELF STATEMENTS. Focus on Other statements refer to a person or group outside the company, and Focus on Self statements focus on people or groups inside the company. It is an external focus versus an internal focus.

The participants were observed throughout their workday for use of these types of statements and the quantities of each statement used. Then the three pairs of statements were evaluated as ratios.

    For this experiment, observers were trained to identify and tally the speech communication patterns. Their task was to watch someone and record the person's use of these specific speech patterns during actual work activities being conducted for real work, on-site at the company facilities.

THE FINDINGS

Once all the data was collected, it was time to see if any patterns emerged. The researchers had (1) a rating of the company performance as high, medium or low based on the study's definition of performance; and (2) reported tallies of the six speech communication patterns of people at each company during a workday. They arranged the tallies into their pre-described ratios and significant patterns emerged. These patterns are their findings. For this study, the findings lead to very specific plays. The plays composing this section of the Playbook are based on how to interpret and apply the numerical ratios - the Math of Extraordinary.

THE MATH OF EXTRAORDINARY™

The results from Losada and Heaphy's study are the communication ratios that predict Extraordinary Performance. A quick analysis reveals two important conclusions when it comes to performance:

- The more you talk about yourself and what you want, the more performance decreases.
- Positivity in how you communicate is associated with high performance.

The plays in this section teach you how to put these ratios in action to create Extraordinary Performance. For me, learning about these ratios has opened the door to what I call The Math of Extraordinary. I need specifics and formulas to guide my behavior, and these ratios do just that. These math ratios are guideposts on the journey to creating an Extraordinary Life.

	Inquiry/Advocacy	Positive/Negative Statements	Other/Self
High Performing	1.14 Inquiry to 1 Advocacy	5.6 Positive to 1 Negative	1 Other to 1.07 Self
Medium Performing	2 Inquiry to 3 Advocacy	1.8 Positive to 1 Negative	1 Other to 1.6 Self
Low Performing	1 Inquiry to 19 Advocacy	1 Positive to 2.7 Negative	1 Other to 29 Self

PLAY #6

THE MAGIC RATIO:
DELIVERING THE POSITIVE

The ratio of 5 positive statements to every 1 negative statement (5+:1-) is magical, unexplainable, and life-changing. Do you want to improve your relationships? Use the 5+:1- ratio. Do you want the creativity to flow? Does your organization want to improve their performance? Put the 5+:1- ratio in motion.

Performance	Number of Statements	
	Positive	Negative
High	5.6	1
Medium	1.8	1
Low	1	2.7

In the study of high to low performing companies, one finding stood out above all the others. The ratio of 5.6 positive statements to each negative statement correlated to a company's performance indicators being high-performing. The statistical analysis confirmed that it wasn't chance or a coincidence with a statistical power of 2. There is a clear, strong connection between this one communication practice and high performance.

This powerful formula for success is not a new discovery. In his relationship research, Dr. John Gottman learned that stable marriages had a ratio of 5 positive statements or signals for every negative one. This discovery has come to be known as Gottman's Ratio. Dr. Gottman's research has become part of mainstream psychology because he was able to predict with 94% accuracy if married couples would still be happily together fifteen years later. His focus was not about attempting to predict divorce rates; he wanted to understand which behaviors predict divorce.

Some people argue that they are different at home than at work, but the Magic Ratio holds true for at work and at home for positive relationships.

A ratio of 5 positives to 1 negative has been found with high performing companies and successful marriages. The research on organizations lets us know that the same dynamic that is a predictor of success in a marriage holds true in all our relationships.

   Our play is a how-to for reaching this ratio whether at home or work. The principles are the same.

THE POSITIVES

The positives are listed as expressing *compliments, approval, appreciation, support, and helpfulness.* When I post this list for my adult students, they immediately roll their eyes and say, "I know someone that must have been in your class and they are such a fake! They are always patting everyone on the back and telling us what a great job we are doing, even when things are miserable." My students are referring to someone that is parroting general statements of positivity. It comes across as condescending and sleazy. They immediately think of the boss that smiles and thanks everyone for showing up and working hard. Clearly this type of positive behavior does not send the right message or count toward the 5 since it results in aggravation instead of inspiration.

DELIVERING POSITIVES HAS TWO COMPONENTS:
* Positive Reinforcement – identifying what you want more of.
* A willingness to connect.

It takes effort and thoughtfulness to do an analysis of what matters and why it matters. Then that information is fed back to the performer in a dialogue that takes time and creates connection. If this is not how you currently talk with people, starting out requires noticing, planning, communicating, and practice!

   The discipline of Human Motor Behavior studies how to help people learn to do or not do behaviors. The key word is learn. When people are growing, they are learning. In your family and at work, part of growth means everyone is learning how to improve skills for better engaging with each other and meeting needs. One of the fundamental principles of learning for improvement is providing what we call knowledge of results regarding what has been done. The 5+:1- ratio provides knowledge of results by providing a stream of information about what is working and needs to be continued or what can be improved.

Human nature focuses on happenings that are bad so we can avoid them in the future. For example, let's say you are walking home about dusk and find a $100 bill on the sidewalk. There's no one around, so it clearly is your good fortune. You pick up the $100 bill and stick it in your wallet. The next day, you take out your wallet to pay for lunch. The $100 bill is still there, but the $5 bill that was there yesterday is gone. That's when you realize that your sense of something hitting the ground when you were putting away the $100 in the dusky light must have been your $5 bill. The research has tested this premise again and again. You'll talk more about the $5 you lost than the $100 you found. It's just how we are wired. It's Mother Nature's way of helping us learn to not make the same mistakes over and over. This focus on avoiding trouble causes us to be blind to the behaviors that are working for us, and we sometimes quit doing something that was a good thing. Good behaviors that are not pointed out and reinforced may not persist.

So, forget the meaningless compliments and automatic yeses. If you learn to reinforce the positives, you'll be providing feedback that counts and builds relationships.

PROVIDING POSITIVE REINFORCEMENT

Positive reinforcement means that you identify something you want more of and let individuals know in a way that gets you more of it. Positive reinforcement that actually builds relationships and creates improved performance has two components. First, the positive feedback describes a specific behavior or action. Second, it puts the behavior in context. Putting the behavior in context means that you explain how the behavior fits in with the big picture to make a difference. It fills the why in this statement:

When you do [the behavior], it makes a difference because of [why].

For instance, as a college instructor, I grade papers that are analyses and reflections on the material and exercises. When my grading primarily points out what the student did incorrectly or what is wrong, my classroom becomes more and more tense as the semester goes along. However, when my grading does the exact same pointing out what is incorrect but also lets the student know what they did well, the classroom retains a tone of learning and success An example of this type of positive feedback to a student would be:

Your example of talking with your roommate, complete with what you did in the past, what you have changed now, and how it has changed your conversation helped me understand your point. I know it takes time to think of examples, but it is worth it to help me understand. You did a great job of telling a story that captured my attention.

When I take the time to provide a detailed level of positive reinforcement for what the student does well at the first of the semester, their work gets better and better in subsequent assignments. The problem is that it takes critical thinking and analysis to determine what provided quality. It's easy to quickly mark what is wrong. Critical thinking requires more than just a yes/no evaluation and has to consider the context. It is hard work.

Providing quality positives takes time and horsepower. It means you think about what someone did and why it mattered. Then you let them know so they can do more of what is working. Some examples for positive reinforcement that will get more of what you want are:

Hi John. We have a departmental due date of Wednesday at noon for everyone's weekly overrun report. You always have your part to me by 8:30 every Wednesday morning. I want you to know that getting it to me first thing on Wednesdays really helps me by providing extra time to think about the numbers so I can give our manager some reasons for our performance. It is a really good thing. Thanks.

Greetings Staff! It's our Monday morning kick-off meeting and I want you to know that our quality numbers inched up a little more last week toward our target. I'm not quite sure why. What do you think happened that helped us be better?

Hi, Honey...When I come in from a trip and you greet me with a smile and some light-hearted stories about what has gone on here at home, it really helps me unwind and forget about the hassles of traveling. I know you could meet me with a list of everything that has gone wrong, but that would make coming home feel like work instead of the best place on earth. I really appreciate it.

Hey kids, thanks for picking up your balls and bats from the yard. I sure would hate to run over your gear with the lawnmower, and it's hard to see it in the high grass. Maybe we can take the money you helped us avoid in unnecessary maintenance and replacing mangled equipment to go someplace fun!

CONNECTING WITH YES

I have a bad habit. I say NO when I really mean WAIT. I like to figure things out. I gather information. I like to be helpful. When someone comes to me and starts to ask about doing something new or different, the first word out of my mouth is frequently – No. Not a mean-spirited No. Just No. What I really mean is, *Wait, I want to change from what I am currently thinking about to listening to you…and it takes me a few seconds to mentally pack away what I am doing so I can give you my attention.*

Unfortunately for me, when NO comes tumbling out, it shuts down the other person. Instead of their conversation flowing out, the other side usually stops and starts again with some sort of rationale in an attempt to prove their point. Then we are into a debate, instead of a discussion.

Just say Yes means that you become incredibly agreeable about hearing other people, their ideas and their information. YES is even better than

WAIT because it invites the other person to lay out their thinking without qualification and measuring their words.

Yes, I am excited to hear what you have to say. Give me two seconds to shift gears so you will have my full attention.

YES doesn't always mean I agree. In delivering the positive,
YES frequently means:

Yes, I hear you.
Yes, that is another way to think about it.
Yes, you might have an insight.
Yes, I am willing to listen to you.

A key habit to develop in delivering the positive is being agreeable about the actual process of engaging. Just say Yes to keep the conversation going. When you do need to deliver a NO, then use the word properly and in context. You will get more engagement when NO is not masquerading as a stop sign. An honest No will sound like:

No, I am not willing to do that because…
I believe your data has a problem and I don't reach the same conclusion.

The point of Yes is that it opens the door to more ideas and more thinking. Using the word No shuts people down, while Yes suggests there is room for more. Use the word Yes every chance you get. Yes responses support the end result, the process, a piece of the idea, or even that there is an idea.

PUTTING THE POSITIVE IN ACTION

Most people want to become better. The odd thing is that we want to make these improvements without anyone else knowing we are working on ourselves! It is as if learning new performance skills is embarrassing. You may be tempted to surreptitiously start using more positives and then see what happens. If you engage in a covert operation of using positives, you will see people respond differently. The changes start immediately.

However, the best way to get started is to let others know you have some new information about being extraordinary, and invite them to come along with you. Who wouldn't want to be successful in relationships?

JUSTIN'S STORY

One of my favorite stories came from a young man in one of my classes. He had a busy job that resulted in long work weeks, a working wife, and two young children. In an energetic burst the year before, he had demolished their kitchen for a remodel. But, work and worries had overtaken him, construction had halted, and he and his wife argued continuously due to the inconvenience of no kitchen and dealing with their children who seemed to grow more needy as the tension between the parents escalated. The new appliances and materials consumed the garage, and toddlers were often found wandering through the kitchen construction zone. The only reason I knew about this was because when I met him two months after our class, he told me about his experience with the power of 5+:1-.

Justin had gone home that night after class and told his wife about the 5+:1- ratio with the high performing companies and Gottman's Ratio for predicting divorce. I honestly believe he recognized that with the way things were going, Gottman would have predicted a divorce in his future. His wife was intrigued and they decided that since they didn't have anything to lose, they would deliberately try it. They started letting the other one know when something good was happening and why, and thanking the other with specifics for helping out. They fell into a strategy of when one of them would be on a negative bend such as frustration with the children, the other would bring up something positive and it would shift the energy. Justin told me that it was amazing – even when he knew she was mechanically providing a positive, it felt good and worked.

Magically, there was energy to finish up the kitchen. The children were calmer. This couple deliberately and purposefully changed their relationship for the better, and it happened in just a couple of months.

ROBIN'S STORY

As a class project, one of my students decided to test the 5+:1- ratio as a solution to a big problem. Robin was the director of the infant nursery for her church. This large church had lots of young families, and was dedicated to providing young parents with childcare during the church service. Robin had a list of 26 vetted and trained volunteers who were scheduled months in advance for five of them to work each Sunday morning. If an attendant couldn't work their assigned slot, they were to call someone else on the list and arrange for a substitute. This plan was not working. Every Sunday there were no-shows with no substitute. Some Sundays, the parents would be forced to stay with their children because of a lack of nursery attendants.

Robin managed the nursery volunteers via email, and she reflected over her style. She decided that her emails were sending a negative message by trying to make the volunteers feel bad about not showing up. She realized that there was no pride in being a nursery volunteer and her attendants weren't getting the message about how much their service in the nursery was an act of love toward the parents.

Robin changed her style. She started sending weekly emails that reminded the workers of how much they mattered. She provided a context that they were providing a gift to their church community. She passed along compliments that parents made when they picked up their kids. She made a list of all the volunteers and systematically began mentioning them by name with a positive attached. She also reminded them to contact someone on the list to arrange a substitute.

Then the magic happened, and it happened immediately. Although her class project due date only allowed for tracking one month's performance, there was perfect attendance from the volunteers, with one exception. One person didn't show up for their assigned slot. Robin told me that something didn't seem right, and when she checked her email, this person had been accidently left off the list of receiving systematic positive reinforcement.

These two stories are not unique. My students are required to run a science experiment to test one of the plays in this book and many of them choose this ratio. I have read about the magic that happens when the positives are put into action hundreds of times. It is easy and it works.

OBSTACLES TO 5+

There are three main obstacles to providing the positives. None of the obstacles has to do with skill or ability. The problem is that, for many of us, reaching the positivity ratio requires changing our thinking.

THE FIRST OBSTACLE is taking the time to engage in critical thinking to notice and then talk with people when we already have too much to do.

THE SECOND OBSTACLE is believing there is value in rewarding what is working.

THE THIRD OBSTACLE is believing that reinforcing the positive is as valuable as noticing problems and getting them fixed.

Providing quality feedback takes time. It takes a pause in running from one task to the next to analyze what is meaningful and why. It takes time to engage in a conversation so you can deliver the positive. The actual time to think and time to deliver a positive is only a couple of minutes. If you think about it, it's not much time at all. The difficulty is it feels like you are being non-productive because it is not task-oriented. You can't look back and see what you accomplished. You'll have to internalize that by spending two minutes engaged in letting people know what works, you'll save those minutes many times over in the future when the good behaviors persist. The cause and effect is not obvious or recordable on a spreadsheet.

I learned about the second obstacle from my adult participants. I have them practice delivering the positive by thinking about what someone at their workplace does that goes unnoticed, but really makes a difference. My students figure out the signal that this good work has happened and what they will say to the person when the signal happens. It doesn't take many report-outs of examples before someone raises their hand and says *I don't think we should be praising people for just doing their job. That's why we hire them and pay them.*

This comment comes from not understanding the true nature of positive reinforcement. The purpose of positive reinforcement is to get more of something. When someone does what you want more of, whether it is their job or not, letting them know how important it is and why will get you more of that behavior. Even when people are doing their job, they have decisions to make about the energy with which they do it and their investment in helping what is downstream and upstream from them even better. It's not about rewarding extremes with compliments. It's about getting more of what you want.

Overcoming the third obstacle requires a shift in personal beliefs. Many of us, especially those of us in strict problem-solving disciplines (you learn more about problem solving disciplines in Play #5: FYI: FI vs FD), have an internal belief that we are most valuable when we are pointing out what is wrong so it can be fixed or avoided. This focus on problem-solving can create a persona of negativity. Being successful at delivering positives requires an additional focus of noticing what was right so you can make sure to replicate what worked. It is a bigger challenge to notice what is working than to notice what isn't. The bad screams for attention. The good isn't a problem, so typical problem solving doesn't work because you are not looking for a culprit. However, the skills used for breaking a problem into pieces so it can be solved are the same ones used to break a good event into pieces. Once you have wrestled with a few good scenarios, it will become another type of problem to solve and wonderful fun.

I asked a group of adult students to come up with ideas for how to immediately implement the 5+:1- ratio. A group of supervisors for a high production line had an idea that all of us can apply in all parts of our lives. This group said that at the end of a shift where everything seemed to go wrong, they always sat down and analyzed the day in an attempt to identify the problem and correct it for the future. Their insight was that at the end of a great day where they hit all their marks, they just smiled and went home. Their action item was that at the end of a great day, they would meet and identify what went well that day so they could make sure the good stuff happened every day.

TIPS ABOUT DELIVERING THE POSITIVE

Can there be too much of a good thing? Research has demonstrated that when the ratio exceeds 10:1, it feels like folks have lost touch with reality. For most of us, delivering 5 solid yeses or positive reinforcements will be a struggle. Remember that the goal is not to deliver as many as possible, the goal is to recognize good and offer a positive for connection. A fun exercise that can help you get a feel for your personal ratio is to put 5 pennies and a nickel in your right pocket. Every time you use a positive, move a penny to the left pocket. When all the pennies have moved, then move them back toward the right. Do the same for the nickel, except move it when you use your negative. You'll get a sense of how often the nickel moves versus the set of 5 pennies.

A great way to notice the positives is to set the *Wow!* signal. The *Wow!* signal is when you see, hear or notice something and inside you get a sense of *Wow!* When you get the *Wow!*, it's time to stop and provide positive reinforcement or at least let them know they made you smile!

PLAY #7

WASTED NEGATIVES:
SARCASM & CYNICISM

The path to Extraordinary Performance starts with the Magic Ratio of 5 positive statements for every 1 negative statement (5+:1-). Mastering this path is a life's work. Frankly, if it's a new concept to you, figuring out how to provide positive reinforcement can require a change in viewpoint. It truly is the cliché of seeing the glass as half-full or half-empty. Either way, the water in the glass is at the same level. The choice is a life-changing decision.

Implementing this ratio of providing so many positives can seem daunting, especially when facing a multitude of faults and problems every day. The quickest method for improving your positive to negative ratio is to stop the frivolous negatives.

The one negative is meant for correcting performance. The purpose of the one negative is to provide useful performance feedback instead of making negative remarks. For example, when someone has a habit that is creating problems for others, use the negative to let them know. If a person has poor skills in an area and needs to improve them, use the one negative to discuss the deficiency.

However, negatives boil out as sarcasm, cynicism, criticism, and disapproval. This type of communication affects the ratio far beyond just creating more negatives than positives. The aftermath of these statements is the creation of a culture of distrust, shutting down, and sabotage that leads to mediocrity or worse.

Sarcasm and its companions are difficult to contain. As our senses take in the actions of others, we are subconsciously programming ourselves to behave the same way. An example of this programming is when you spend time with people that use a different vocabulary, you'll find yourself suddenly using those words. For me, if I spend time with people using inappropriate words, next thing I know, those offensive words bounce out when I am teaching!

What we see, hear, and read subconsciously programs our actions. When exposed to bad habits, we adopt them without even trying. We are deluged with sarcasm and negativity by the media, both television and online. This steady diet of nastiness makes it OK to use sarcasm and become cynical.

Eliminating sarcasm, cynicism, criticism, and disapproval from your interactions drastically changes your personal ratio of positive to negative, because every time you use one of these negative statements, you need five positives to offset it. However, it's not clear that the positives work to directly rebalance your message. These statements generate internalized distrust and emotional responses. It takes a long time to shift someone's internal perception of you.

If using these negative statements is your habit, the first step to eliminating them is to understand their origins, what they sound like, and their impact on performance.

SARCASM

Sarcasm is defined as apparent praise that actually has a different meaning which is scornful and mocking. It ridicules while the actual words appear to be nice. Sarcasm often is put forth as being funny due to the twist of niceness that actually is cutting and mean. Sarcasm is fun for the people who are not the targets because it is a sort of puzzle and brain-teaser. High quality sarcasm will use just a few words to imply a lot of opposite meaning. It is never clear as to exactly what the sarcastic statement means, and the puzzle of it all is a game for many people until the remarks are turned toward them.

Here's my definition of sarcasm. Sarcasm is shoving without touching. What I mean by shoving without touching is that when someone is in my way physically or not doing what I want them to do, I attempt to get them to move or change by shoving them with words.

My first professional job was with a government contractor. I was fresh out of engineering school and really didn't know a lot about the working world. Within the first few days, my boss had a conversation with me about basic rules of the workplace. He told me that there were two things to never do. First, never steal anything. He told me that engineers continue their love of tinkering at home and are always working on something. He told me to never take home a tool for a weekend project, even if I was going to bring it back. He told me not to take so much as a cheap government supplied pen or pencil home. There was always a chance that someone would visit my house, see a government issued item, call the FBI, and accuse me of stealing government property. He said, "Don't steal because they won't ask questions. You'll be fired and could go to jail for stealing government property. Plus, it's not worth losing your job and ruining your reputation for a tool or a cheap pen."

Then he told me the second rule to never break. My boss said, "Never hit anyone. If you hit someone, they will take you right out of here." I have yet to meet someone that says this workplace rule has changed. We still don't allow hitting in the workplace. So, since we can't hit or shove those people that are holding us up or are in our way, we do it with words. We attempt to get them to move, leave us alone, or change their behavior with words. Believe me, there would be a lot less sarcasm if hitting were allowed (a little humor here...)!

Needless to say, I made sure to never hit anyone or steal anything. And just as he described, those employees unfortunate enough to break these rules were immediately escorted out of the gate.

Here's the problem with sarcasm. You say one thing and mean another. It is a form of lying as it misrepresents the truth. Sarcasm can seem funny when the target is not you or someone you care about. But, a sarcastic statement is an attack on the target plus those people who are aligned with the target. It is as if someone hid behind a bush and stuck out a 2x4 board to trip another person passing by...and everybody who was watching laughed. Sarcasm makes fun of people, and the bystanders that laugh become part of the negative vibe.

Trustworthiness is a foundation quality for connecting with people in a way that creates value. Trust is demonstrated by openness, reliability, and compassion. Compassion requires a willingness to connect. Reliability means you can depend on someone. Openness is based on a sense of safety in the relationship. Sarcasm strikes a blow at all of these qualities. People are not willing to be open or connect to someone that does not say what they mean, and saying one thing while meaning another is the very definition of sarcasm. Sarcasm has an element of confusion as sarcastic words can be interpreted in different ways, thus damaging reliability. Trust and mean-spiritedness are never companions.

If your words and actions are not straightforward and accurate, then you don't know what message the other party and the bystanders received. Sarcasm covertly creates enemies and shuts people down. It's a nasty habit for avoiding honest dialogue.

So, here's a short quiz for you. On most days, by lunch time, how many sarcastic statements and comments have you made? Take a guess. Then multiply that by 5 and you have the number of positive statements you owe to bring the balance sheet to Extraordinary Performance. However, with sarcasm, it's doubtful that the ratio works in the short term. People, especially those that are watching from the sidelines, need a sustained experience of positive behaviors to internalize that you are really trustworthy.

When I talk about sarcasm in my adult classes, I can count on someone coming up to me at the break and saying, "My whole family is sarcastic. That's how we talk. This can't be true because we all stick together. That's just our way." My best response came from another student (and I've heard this more than once) who said, "A friend's family is incredibly sarcastic, and she talks like that all the time. My family is never sarcastic. After visiting her house a few times, I told her that I wasn't going back because the way her family talked was mean…and I thought she was mean to other people. I also let her know that if she continued to be so sarcastic, I didn't want to hang out with her anymore."

The next time you hear someone make a sarcastic remark, take a quick look around the room to see who seems uncomfortable or is not laughing. The battle lines are being drawn for not cooperating, connecting, and sharing information in an invisible war.

The best way to deal with sarcasm is to disarm the guilty party by taking away their weapon. People who are sarcastic say one thing, hoping that people get a different message than the words transmit. To counter sarcasm, become very literal. Once you take their comment at face value, it won't make sense to you. Then you ask them to explain what they meant.

Many years ago I was on an off-site assignment on the West Coast and my home office was in East Tennessee. I often needed to discuss strategy with my team back in Tennessee and the open cubical arrangement at my remote office didn't allow any privacy. So, I would get up early and talk to the home office. It would be 7 am for me and 10 am for my team back home. Many mornings I would arrive at my West Coast office about 9 am. I had been working, but remotely. A man in my office decided that I was simply sleeping late and showing up to work whenever I wanted. One morning when I arrived at my desk about 9:15, he blurted out, loud enough for the entire office to hear, "So, I see you are bringing in the evening paper again." This old cliché is meant to embarrass the person who is late by calling attention to them as if they are coming in so late that the afternoon paper has been published. I took his statement at face value and replied to him, "I don't know what you mean by that statement. Can you please explain it?"

He turned bright red and stomped away to the coffee pot. He left me alone after my question, but I know I made an enemy. No amount of explanation was going to change his mind, but I stopped the public harassment. I stopped his acting out, but not his thought process. He had already become cynical.

CYNICISM

Being cynical means that you are critical and distrusting of the motives of others. Other words that are associated with cynicism are peevish and sneering...neither of which are compliments about behavior.

Cynical people are suspect of everything that happens. When the company offers an unexpected bonus, they are the ones that say, "So, I guess this bonus is in lieu of a raise so the front office doesn't have to increase our base pay." Cynicism does not take happenings at face value. It finds a reason that whatever has happened is actually negative.

What we repeatedly experience with our senses changes our brain. Repeated patterns of mental activity build neural structure and the patterns of thinking we establish become our preferred way of responding. People with a long history of cynicism change the physical structure of their brain. Thus, the more you find the negative, the better you get at seeing it. The more your interpretation of life is about negative motives, the more your way of thinking about life will be one of distrust and unfair treatment. Then, seeing the negative becomes the default response. For the cynical, their glasses are not rose-colored or clear. They see the world through a lens of gray where everything is dark and getting darker.

Happiness and contentment depend on having a base sense of safety, satisfaction, and connection. The more a person sees threats, the more their brain spends time in reactive mode, and the person lives with an escalating sense of distrust and stress.

THIS IS A GOOD TIME TO ASK YOURSELF:
- When does cynicism creep into your evaluation of what is happening?
- Are your responses a true analysis of the facts or are they based on what you suspect to be ulterior motives based on your insider information?

One of the most common questions from my adult students as we discuss wasted negatives is how to deal with incredibly cynical people. For these extreme naysayers, cynicism is a chronic condition where it feels impossible to make progress on any subject because of the focus on unresolvable issues and motives.

A mistake in working with a cynic is to prepare a logical argument to disprove their position. A second mistake is to engage in sarcasm and cynicism that pokes back at them. Neither of these two strategies will work. The cynic is not basing their viewpoint on logic. It is a perspective based on searching for what might be negative. Cynicism is not based on rational thought and no amount of logical discussion is likely to change the mind and responses of the cynic. It is how they have decided to see the world. Everything is colored by unknowns that have negative implications.

Cynicism can be a result when an organization promises one thing, but then doesn't deliver. When individuals believe they have been treated unfairly, one response is to distrust the motives of the other party. The same holds true among individual relationships. The antidote to cynicism is resiliency.

RESILIENCY

In the field of personal development, *Resiliency* is how people handle adversity and positively adapt. Some research has suggested that cynicism is an outgrowth of promises being made and not kept. It can fester when people see unfair treatment or when plans fail. The cynic has decided to believe that what will transpire is out of their control.

Resiliency is being able to make positive adjustments to negative happenings and is part of developmental growth. People who experience negativity yet emerge still focused on opportunities and positivity tend to have support systems such as other individuals and resources that lessen the impact of the unfortunate event. It is thought that when bad things or disappointments happen to a person, they have a choice. One choice is to see opportunities or perhaps decide to overlook the bad event, and with this choice they continue their personal growth. This decision to move on indicates personal resiliency. If the person takes the other choice and decides that life is unfair, they are likely to become cynical and personal growth comes to a halt. Personal growth is believed to come about based on a positive response to a bad event or disappointment.

Cynics may have suffered unduly at some point due to no fault of their own, and continue their defensiveness by a heightened distrust. Regardless of how the cynic came to be created, or the extent to which they have adopted a perspective of doubt and distrust, changing the perspective of the cynic requires a consistent program designed to improve resiliency. It is not a single conversation, a move to a new position, or a threat about action if attitudes do not change.

Building trust takes a sustained environment where people do what they say and openness is welcomed. In working with cynics, it takes time for their thought processes to remap. Trust is built on common experiences, and the easy way out by logical explanations just doesn't work.

Sometimes, it takes time for a cynic to bounce back. In a Leadership class for supervisors, one of my star performers, Jim, offered up his own story when we started talking about cynicism and its problems. He talked about how he has been a really hard worker as a young man, and was promised a promotion several times. But, due to an economic downturn and then a change in contracts, he was never promoted. It seemed there was always someone already in a management role that needed to be relocated. Jim started to believe that good work had nothing to do with getting ahead and that he was being treated unfairly. Jim said that he became cynical and was critical and miserable to both himself and those around him. Time passed and his young family started growing. He said that one day, he heard his young daughter mimic his cynical attitude. Then he realized the damage his bitterness was causing and that he didn't want to be stuck anymore. He deliberately changed jobs and adopted his old attitude of hard work and positivity. It wasn't long until he was back on track and promoted. He took action to get back on the path of personal growth.

There are two lessons in Jim's story about dealing with cynics. First, Jim was treated unfairly by an overall economic change and then by how his company changed. It wasn't personal, but he didn't get what had been promised. He let it get the best of him when things didn't ever go back to when he had been in favor. Lesson One is that bad things happen to good people and promises are broken. Many people don't start out cynical, but can become distrustful and marginally productive. Lesson Two is that Jim decided on his own to bounce back and be resilient. It wasn't from what someone did for him or finally getting an explanation. He summoned the courage to change how he looked at life.

Logic, a new promotion, or something said by the boss doesn't change the cynic. Change is a decision they have to make for themselves. It is a change in perspective and not a change in skill set. That is what makes it so difficult to overcome.

ELIMINATING SARCASM AND CYNICISM

In my teaching and coaching, many very kind and well-meaning people are shocked to learn about the impact that Sarcasm and Cynicism have on relationships and organizations. They start off being quite defensive and talk about how they use these two communication techniques to keep people laughing. They believe that sarcasm, in particular, is a great way to build comradery. They talk about how it's just a way of talking and everyone knows that it is not intended to be mean. Once the defensiveness passes, my students start to understand that sarcasm is not funny to everyone and it's never clear who is backing away.

For my adult students, they usually come back to me in a few weeks with the realization of the damage that sarcasm does. They realize that it is not straightforward and is a habit that needs to be changed if they intend to be seen as someone who is trustworthy and kind. They learn to make jokes only about themselves, and find that it is easier to be honest than to attempt to get things to happen by poking others with sarcasm.

Unfortunately, in the case of working with cynics, there is not an easy solution. It is more than changing a bad habit. Cynicism is a perspective, and is not changed by simply pointing out the damage done. Cynics believe that how they are seeing the world is how it really is. A cynical person will most likely be known for saying that they are just telling it like it is whether everyone else likes it or not. For most people problems, there is advice on how to help them change. For dealing with a cynic, the advice is to never hire one. There is no formula for changing them. There is no guarantee you can change their perspective, especially since it means they will need to stop interpreting actions as unfair treatment and proactively get on the bandwagon of personal growth. Plus, damage is done to those around them from a running commentary on how things are bad and getting worse.

Sarcasm and Cynicism are wasted negatives. They use up the negative side of the Magic Ratio in a way that doesn't help people improve. Using sarcasm is a bad habit, and cynicism casts a cloud over the entire group, whether it be friends, family, or at work. If you use sarcasm, the quickest way to improve your ratio is to stop saying things differently than they actually are by becoming straightforward. If you are a cynic, you'll need to decide to give personal growth another try and to decide that, just maybe, not everyone and every organization deserves distrust of their motives. Sometimes people just make mistakes and regrettable things happen.

PLAY #8

DELIVERING THE ONE
(OF THE 5+:1- RATIO)

It seems most people dread having to deliver negative messages. They anticipate damaging relationships, creating ill will, and engaging in conflict. But, what if you conceptualize *Delivering the One* as helping people along their path? I like to think that we are together on a journey up a mountain. The path is steep, narrow, and full of hazards. If I see someone about to have problems, I offer a hand. I do my best to keep them from stumbling or falling down the mountain. Providing feedback that helps people become better is the same as helping them along a difficult journey. When the Magic Ratio is working, negatives become a helping hand instead of criticism.

Once the non-value-added sarcasm, cynicism, criticism, defensiveness, and disapproving statements have been eliminated, there is the one acceptable negative: it is a correction. It's helpful to sort the types of correction into categories:

- An improvement to performance that is already good
- A change to performance that is not so good
- A change in performance to meet required standards

Once you learn the technique for Delivering the One Negative, the steps are the same for all corrections regardless of the category.

THREE KEY INSIGHTS

Delivering the One starts with embracing three important fundamental concepts about how to deliver feedback. The three fundamentals are: (1) applying the 8% rule, (2) determining if the type of feedback is an improvement or a required change and (3) understanding the role of the 5 positives.

ELAINE'S LAW OF 8%

Elaine's Law of 8% is crucial for success with *Delivering the One*. Elaine's Law of 8% says that about 8% of people have no intention of working with others and creating Extraordinary Performance (*Elaine's Law of 8%* is described in detail in the section Playbook: General Rules). They are the folks who are cynical and impede forward motion with their venom based on distrust. They are the folks that are distracted by other things in their life and don't pull their weight, both as a member of the group and in accomplishing their tasks. The 8% accounts for about 90% of problems. Skills training does not fix the problem. Threats and formal corrective action only drives them underground or provides a temporary fix. This play for *Delivering the One* doesn't work on them. My plea with you is to not abandon the play because you tried it on the 8%. If you will use this play with everybody else, the ones that are just waiting to improve, it's amazing how fast things change.

COACHING AND COUNSELING

The second fundamental came as an Ah-Ha! moment for me. In hindsight, I was not a very good supervisor in my engineering career. I attribute the majority of my difficulties to ignorance of a fundamental concept of providing feedback. Unfortunately for all of those people who reported to me, I learned this fundamental concept long after I left engineering and management when I began teaching a basic leadership course.

My boss at the University of Tennessee asked me to begin teaching an undergraduate leadership course. She handed me a textbook and said, "I have used this book with MBA students. It might be a nice starting place for you." So the first semester I taught the course, I used the textbook as my guide and stayed a couple of chapters ahead of the class in preparing my formal instruction.

The chapter on providing performance feedback had two pages about a fundamental concept that explained why being a manager had been so difficult for me. This concept explained the difference between coaching and counseling. Management theory splits giving feedback into two categories. One category is termed Coaching. Coaching is helping people improve. It can be improving skills for better performance to a standard. It can be working with someone to improve their personal skills so they become a more valuable employee.

My favorite image of coaching is of the fathers that coached my middle school girls' softball team. These men hit countless grounders and fly balls to a group of girls from the time we were nine years old until we were 14. They spent hours in structured practice and underhanded thousands of pitches for us to hit. They gave each of us individual attention to improve our weak spots. They pushed us, encouraged us, and were as much a part of the experience as the team's players.

Coaches tell us what to do so we can be better performers. Then they provide feedback on our attempts to implement the changes. And, they celebrate when we get it right. Whether you are a teacher, parent, friend, manager, mentor, or a fellow employee, you can be a coach to those around you. One of the best ways to build long-lasting relationships is to be a coach. Coaches see who you are now and offer you a glimpse of who you might be. Great coaches help you figure out a way to get there.

The other category of feedback is Counseling. Counseling happens when disciplinary action is put into motion. The person has no choice. Rules have been broken, and if changes are not made to meet the rules, the discipline will escalate. There is no choice and the path forward is clear. At work, the processes for Counseling scenarios are outlined in company procedures. At home, the severity of the consequences escalates as the problem behaviors persist.

Here's why this was an Ah-Ha! moment for me. I did not understand the difference between Coaching and Counseling. The feedback I gave my employees came across backward, so it sent the wrong message. When I say backward, I talked about opportunities in a way that sounded rigid, while I talked about disciplinary action as if it was a choice. When I went to talk with a young engineer about learning a new piece of software because it would make them more versatile, I used the tone of Counseling to do it. So instead of being encouraging, talking about the benefits, and how it fit in with their career potential, I made them anxious about if their skills were adequate. When I dealt with a difficult employee who was chronically late, I softened it first by talking about their potential to do good work and how important they were. They didn't get the message that there was no option when it came to their being on time. They probably figured being late didn't matter because they had just received encouragement for doing such good work.

After frequently making my good people angry with my misguided attempts to provide opportunities, and making no apparent progress with those people who had true disciplinary problems, I gave up and retreated to my office. It seemed I could not get anything right. My group wasn't moving forward, and dealing with my few disciplinary problems dominated my day. I dreaded any conversation with my employees and internalized all feedback as an upcoming fight.

When I read the difference between Coaching and Counseling, I immediately understood what had happened. I should have dropped in on my good employees to talk about the future for our department and to let them know what I believed they could accomplish with some deliberate learning of new skills and opportunities to practice those skills. The conversation should have been a coaching dialogue about what they believed and what I observed. It should have been a conversation about what is your next goal and how might you get there. Working with these employees should have been as much fun for me as it was for the softball dads watching their little girls grow and become seasoned competitors.

I also understood where I should have used Counseling. I recalled situations when one of my good employees would fall into a bad habit, and before my corrective conversation was over, everyone was mad. I was pleading with them and sent a cluttered message, when the prescribed course of action should have been a simple, calm conversation that reminded them of expectations, and that the next step would start formal action. The good employees would have been upset that their actions had resulted in this type of feedback, but, the correction would have been immediate, and soon they would of been back working to become a more valued employee.

I recalled a few employees in the 8% that were never influenced by begging, pleading or kindness. I had to summon a tremendous amount of energy to enter into a black and white discussion of expectations, and how they would be held accountable. To me, it seemed as if it was my fault the conversation was happening at all.

The lesson here is to evaluate the feedback you have to deliver. If the feedback helps people get better or understand more opportunities and how to get there, it is probably coaching. If it is coaching, put on your smile, gather up your positive energy and get ready to have some fun.

If the feedback is about rules that have been broken – gather your evidence as quickly as possible, meet privately, and be clear and direct about what has happened and the next step. Although you don't have to wear a frown, this is serious business and deserves a matter-of-fact demeanor.

THE 5 POSITIVES

Delivering the One works in combination with the other side of the ratio – the 5 positives. When the focus is on providing feedback about what is working so everyone can do more of it, the one negative becomes about improving so there is even more success.

Naysayers often make fun of the 5+:1- ratio saying that it is seeing things through rose-colored glasses while ignoring what's wrong. This thinking is absolutely incorrect. Properly applied, feedback about a problem is provided immediately and it doesn't have to be a big deal. Application of the ratio means that there is a steady stream of reinforcing what is working, and a dialog about how to become even better.

Once you neutralize the 8% of resisters, Delivering the One starts to repair the nagging problems and to create a high performance team or family unit. When the ratio is reversed and there are more negatives than positives, negative feedback fosters an atmosphere of failure and your few positive comments are lost in a sea of compliance, mediocrity, and frustration.

You have two choices. Using the 5+:1- ratio, you polish up the rough spots on the diamond. When the ratio is reversed, you can hunt all day for the diamond in a chunk of coal but you won't find it. Either way, you have a chunk of coal. The application of the 5+:1- ratio is what creates and polishes the diamond.

THE 3-STEP PROCESS FOR DELIVERING THE ONE

There is no doubt that providing honest observations and feedback can feel like opening a can of worms, but the 3-step process in this play will help you become a beloved coach who is clearly focused on taking the team to Extraordinary Performance.

The #1 mistake made in giving negative feedback is mixing in some good things in an attempt to make the problem not seem bad. Many of us have a sense that people get angry at any correction, and we try to soften the blow by adding in extra information about their good qualities that clutters up the message. Unfortunately, the primary problem with giving negative feedback is talking about other topics. The not-so-clear feedback then doesn't facilitate change, and the receiver doesn't know exactly what is happening. The result is a twinge of distrust and uncertainty. A simple fix-up can quickly deteriorate into a blow-up.

As difficult as it is to initiate discussions about negative behaviors and performance, people deserve to know. However, think about negative feedback this way. If you have a habit that annoys your fellow workers, would you rather everyone talk behind your back about how annoying you are, or would you rather someone tell you? Yes, it might be embarrassing, but which alternative is worse? Would you rather hear some feedback about how to improve or continue making the same mistakes?

I have read many processes and plans for delivering negative feedback. I was never able to put a system for delivering feedback into practice until I learned this 3-step process. The systems had either too many steps or the steps were not laid out with clear definitions so I could apply them like a formula. This simple three-step process is clear. The courage to be honest and straightforward about negative events is the difficult part.

Dr. Kim Cameron provides a three-step process for providing feedback. I believe this simple formula provides a structure for giving clear, direct feedback that helps people get better. I encourage you to commit these three steps to memory. An insight from my own application and teaching of these steps is to avoid embellishing them. More is not better. Take the steps at face value and prepare a concise message. Most times, delivering negative feedback isn't a dialogue – it is information delivered and perhaps clarified with a resulting focus on generating alternatives for improvement.

STEP 1: DESCRIBE YOUR OBSERVATION OF THE EVENT/BEHAVIOR THAT NEEDS TO BE MODIFIED. Have evidence. If the feedback is about a bad behavior, find the time to observe it so you can provide an example of when you saw this occur. If it is an action tied to a standard, gather data or observe performance of the action to provide evidence of the problem behavior. People become defensive when the conversation is hearsay about a problem. You'll come across as accusatory and critical without an example. Having a standard for comparison changes the game. It is a must. It makes the feedback not be a personal attack.

- Don't wait to say something until you have built up a lot of emotion from being annoyed. Sometimes the person giving the feedback has to get up their nerve to approach someone to Deliver the One. Plus, the longer you wait, the more embarrassed and upset the person is likely to become when they learn they have a problem behavior. If you need to deliver bad news, do it quickly. If you are offering a better way to do a task, then let the person know right away so their reputation is not put at risk.

- Describe emotions as facts. When you put a word on an emotion, it turns it into a fact that can be discussed.

GOOD PRACTICE – Pete, I saw your anger at ...
GOOD PRACTICE – Joyanna, I noticed that you were nervous and your voice was shaky at the start of the presentation.

- Compare what you saw or the measured results to a standard. It's important that the feedback is not your opinion, but that it is being compared to a standard of performance or behavior. When you provide feedback based on opinions, you open yourself up to being seen as playing favorites.

- Identify behaviors that anyone would agree upon. *Too much*, and *not enough* are general descriptions and are your opinion instead of a specific conclusion that would be agreed upon by anyone.

GOOD PRACTICE – Tim, I can hear your speaker phone conversations across the room, even at my desk. It disrupts other conversations and makes it difficult for me to concentrate.

POOR PRACTICE – Tim, you are talking too loud when you use your speaker phone for conversations.

- Avoid talking about motives. It seems to be easier when we can blame a behavior on a motive. We feel that having a reason will make it easier to problem-solve or take action. A discussion of motives is a guess and opens the door for misunderstanding.

POOR PRACTICE – Tim, I can hear your speaker phone conversations across the room, even at my desk. It disrupts other conversations and makes it difficult for me to concentrate. I know you are using the speaker phone so you have both hands to type notes while talking. (This example starts with the previous good practice and then by adding a motive, turns it to poor practice. Additionally, adding on the motive makes giving the feedback more work and clutters the message.)

GOOD PRACTICE – Jeff, I have the production report from last week and the data indicates that you were 10% short of the required amount of samples to process every day.

POOR PRACTICE – Jeff, I have the production report from last week and the data indicates that you were 10% short of the required amount of samples to process every day. I think you were busy flirting with the new hire and it kept you from making your production numbers.

STEP 2: DESCRIBE YOUR REACTION TO THE BEHAVIOR AND THE RESULTING CONSEQUENCES. Regardless of the type of correction, this step is the same. Whether your reaction is one of being surprised, thrilled, frustrated or sad, you reflect on your personal emotional response to what has happened. Be prepared to let the person know the fallout, both emotionally and to the task, as a result of their behavior.

AN IMPROVED GOOD PRACTICE – Tim, I can hear your speaker phone conversations across the room, even at my desk. It causes me to be frustrated because I can't focus on my work when I am doing something tedious. It disrupts other conversations and makes it difficult for me to concentrate.

POOR PRACTICE – Tim, it's really bad when you use your speaker phone. We can't think because you are too loud.

AN IMPROVED GOOD PRACTICE – Joyanna, I am concerned that your audience did not get the message you were delivering today in your presentation. I noticed that you were nervous and your voice was shaky at the start of the presentation. I believe you have an important career ahead of you, and giving presentations becomes even more important as your responsibilities grow.

STEP 3: DEVELOP ALTERNATIVES. Once you have explained the problem behavior, how you feel about it and the consequences, move on quickly to alternatives to repair it. Possible alternatives can be formal training; help from an associate to demonstrate and show the person how a task can be performed to standards; or a discussion of expectations and how performance will be measured. It's important to focus on the behavior, because behaviors can be fixed. If you start a dialogue about the person, then it may quickly become about a trait or characteristic that can't be changed and the person will feel attacked.

ALL 3 STEPS TOGETHER – Joyanna, I am concerned that your audience did not get the message you were delivering today in your presentation. I noticed that you were nervous and your voice was shaky at the start of it. I believe you have an important career ahead of you, and giving presentations becomes even more important as your responsibilities grow. What would you think about going to a class on presentation skills to improve your skills? What other activities do you think might be helpful?

ALL 3 STEPS TOGETHER – Tim, I become frustrated when you use your speaker phone on calls. Hearing your conversation in the background makes it impossible for me to focus on my work or pay attention to other people if I am having a conversation. What can be done so that you can have the conversations you need and I don't have the distraction?

POOR PERFORMANCE WITH CONFUSION ABOUT PERCEIVED PERFORMANCE AND ESCALATION OF EMOTION – Tim, you are a really great guy. You do great work and handle our vendor's demands really well. However, you are driving me crazy using your speaker phone, and others are complaining too. It is loud and we can't think. It seems you don't really care about us because if you did, you'd be more considerate.

(Tim's response) Maybe the reason I do such good work is that I have my hands free to take notes and shuffle around in the contracts. I'd wear headphones with a microphone, but you know it is company policy that we can't wear headphones. So what do you want? Great work or a nice quiet workplace? Plus, Kara across the aisle uses her speaker phone all the time just so she can talk and do her nails. I haven't heard you disciplining her!

Josh, one of my adult students, let me know of his experience using the three steps. He started by letting me know that he did not like conflict, and in the past had avoided giving any feedback that might cause a flare-up of emotion. He had avoided giving all three types of correction, and had difficulty building connections with his employees. He was excited to let me know how the 3-Step approach to Delivering the One had worked in a difficult situation.

Josh told me that he had two top-notch employees. These two men carried the weight of accomplishing the most difficult work and also recognizing problem areas because of their experience. Josh said that the two of them became angry at each other over something that had nothing to do with work and neither was willing to talk to the other. Each of them had individually complained to him about the other. He believed that they had decided to draw a line in the sand and stick to it.

Josh had no choice but to address their sudden inability to work together. It was affecting the group's performance. Josh didn't have a better idea, so he planned out his speech and Delivered the One using the 3-Step approach. I asked Josh what he did for the 3-Steps and from what he relayed to me, he called both of them into his office and the conversation went something like this.

STEP 1: Fellows, I've been watching you and I've noticed that the two of you can't seem to work together anymore on big problems. You don't share information, and you ignore each other. You both have talked to me about the other with complaints. (Notice, Josh described what he had observed and no mention of motives.)

STEP 2: I don't know what happened, but I am disappointed that you can't work out your differences. You have a long history of being friends and working on tough problems together. Now we aren't providing our usual great work and enjoying what we do. (Josh described his feelings about their behavior and the consequences of their behavior.)

STEP 3: You can either work it out right now in front of me or decide to get over it. Either way, this disagreement stops now and you are going to get along with each other. (Josh didn't give them much opportunity to generate their own alternatives, but did layout a plan of what was to happen next.)

If your personal style is to talk a lot in these conversations to attempt to get things fixed without hurting any feelings, it doesn't work. If your style is to just wait around for things to work themselves out, it may be a very long wait with lots of damage in the meanwhile.

Good people can sometimes get off on the wrong track. People with great potential sometimes don't know what their next step should be in development. Many times, people don't even recognize their potential to approach others about next steps. When you are delivering a continual stream of positives, Delivering the One simply becomes a course correction or an improvement. Not a big deal.

The 3-Step process is to the point, neat, and clean. First, describe what happened in relation to expected standards. Second, let them know how you feel about it and the consequences of their actions. Third, come up with alternatives that get people back on track or moving to the next level.

PLAY #9

THE RATIO FOR CREATING:
INQUIRY VS. ADVOCACY

The second ratio from the communication research informs us how to deliberately construct high performance with the ratio of Inquiry statements to Advocacy statements. Inquiry statements are those that ask your counterparts what they think, while advocacy statements are telling what you think and arguing/supporting someone else. Inquiry is asking and Advocacy is selling.

The researchers observed 1.14 Inquiry statements for every 1 Advocacy statement in high performing organizations. The ratio was 1 Inquiry statement for every 1.5 Advocacy statements for medium performance, and 1 Inquiry statement to every 19 Advocacy statements for low performance. There was more Inquiry than Advocacy associated with high performance, and more Advocacy than Inquiry in medium and low performing companies.

	Number of Statements	
Performance	Inquiry	Advocacy
High	1.14	1
Medium	2	3
Low	1	19

A good rule of thumb is that there should be about 1 Inquiry statement for each Advocacy statement. There should be about the same amount of asking for other's opinions as selling your own.

When Inquiry statements equal Advocacy statements, the end result is exploration, discovery and arriving at new ideas through open dialogue supporting ideas. It is the Math of the Extraordinary's Magic Ratio for reaching creative solutions.

INQUIRY STATEMENTS

Inquiry statements explore, and with exploration comes discovery. These statements explore the content and facts, and they can explore how people feel about ideas and concepts. You don't have to create a new list of inquiry statements for every topic or encounter. A great play is to have questions you can use to invite people to participate regardless of the topic. Open-ended invitations such as What do you think? are often too broad. Examples of general purpose statements that can become part of your standard scripts are:

I know you have experience with [*the topic*]. Tell me what you are thinking. Jeff, we haven't heard your take on [*the topic*]. What are a couple of things that stand out to you?

I want everyone to jot down their two most exciting thoughts about our problem. Then let's hear the 30 second version from each person. Once we get the ideas out, then we can start asking questions. *How is this like what we have done before? How is this not like what we have done before?*

ADVOCACY STATEMENTS

Advocacy statements sell and support the speaker's position.

Here's what I think we should do.
I'm in agreement with Cheryl that we should...

The research tells us that others want to hear us and our ideas about the same amount as they want to be heard. In the actual study that produced the Math of the Extraordinary ratios, the researchers include the phrase argue for as a description of advocacy. Whether argue for means an emotional, tense argument or endorsing, expect passion when it comes to putting yourself out there with your ideas or supporting the ideas of others. Advocacy statements that can be part of your general script are:

There are some points/features I really like about Nathan's plan and here's why. I have been thinking about our problem and have some ideas. Let me put the ideas out there and then I'd like to hear your feedback (actually combines advocacy and inquiry).I have a suggestion. How about I put it out for consideration?

CREATING WITH OTHERS

Imagine that you are in a meeting. It is going well with people sharing ideas, supporting ideas, and asking Yes, how might we accomplish […]. You look around the table and realize that a few people haven't said much. Some seem frustrated as evidenced by the scowl on their face, and some seem interested. However, none of these folks are offering their ideas and insights. Equal parts Inquiry and Advocacy counts the types of statements made, and also includes everyone having equal opportunity to participate.

It's time to put your lion tamer suit on, and pick up your chair and whip. You are about to enter the big cat cage complete with lions, tigers and a fiery ring for leaping through. Your task is to get those people that are busy talking and energetically running over each other to be calm for a bit and pause, to provide the opportunity for the ones that aren't participating to give their ideas and information. You become the lion tamer. It will help you to have a visual of entering the center of the ring, taking the whip and chair and putting the big cats up on their stands to sit calmly. You'll keep the chair pointed at them while turning to the non-participants and with a little flick of the whip and an inviting voice, coax them to get off their stands and jump through the fiery ring. You make it safe for them to engage by keeping the others at bay.

The vision of you as a lion tamer sets the tone for your confidence and quick responses to those trying to circle around your back for an attack. It also gives you the pacing to keep the impatient big cats calm while everyone takes their turn at doing tricks.

The goal is to enforce as much asking for opinions and information as selling your own ideas. The target is an even balance between here's what I think and the exploration of what do you think?

People are all unique. We are a combination of what we believe creates success, our preferences in engaging with others, and execution of the plan vs. thinking of more possibilities. When the big cats are all in the ring, each one is going at the discussion from the way they believe will best create success. When they all talk at once, some people get fired up and others shut down. Some want to run with the first idea while others continue to generate new possibilities.

In your lion tamer role, you set the structure for today's act, get everyone in their places, and orchestrate a performance where everyone does their part. You must insist on Inquiry and Advocacy.

OBSTACLES TO 1:1 INQUIRY/ADVOCACY

There are three main obstacles to successfully achieving a 1:1 ratio of Inquiry to Advocacy. The obstacles are independent of each other, but all lead to more Advocacy than Inquiry and resulting decreased performance.

The first obstacle is stonewalling, one of the four relationship killers. Stonewalling is when people are non-responsive to what others are saying. The stonewaller may sit passively without any non-verbal cues that suggest they are listening or engaged. They don't provide non-verbals that provide a clue as to their take on the conversation. They avoid and hunker down.

In defense of stonewallers, sometimes the environment is not safe for them to engage. Another person in the room might have a history of stealing ideas. The tension in the room may create a sense that no one is really listening. The energy in the room may create such a hectic pace, the stonewaller feels left behind.

Regardless of the reason, stonewalling and not engaging, at best, misses a great opportunity to build relationships and, at worst, leaves a negative impression and destroys relationships. Stonewallers wear out other people by forcing the group to spend energy attempting to draw them out. To other people, working with a stonewaller feels like pushing a rope – you can push all day; you can push fast and you can push slow, but you don't get anywhere. The group soon moves on and leaves the stonewaller behind.

The second obstacle is a misunderstanding of what quality listening is. Quality listening is half of a dialogue composed of speaking and listening. Being forced to sit while other people drone on and on is not listening. To listen means that you are not talking and, instead, you are paying attention and absorbing what others are saying. The problem is that the definition of listening doesn't address a dialogue. We often think that being a good listener means we say less and less. Listening is just one side of the dialogue. The goal is to have the skills to engage in a quality dialogue.

Done well, a dialogue is a fun challenge. It means you are paying attention to non-verbals and words to get a deep understanding of what the person means. It is Dynamic Listening in action. A dialogue with Inquiry and Advocacy in mind means there is an equal amount of asking and exploring the other person's thoughts to stating what you think and support. The Inquiry/Advocacy Ratio is about dialogue.

The third obstacle is cynicism. The Inquiry/Advocacy Ratio depends on trust that all parties are open to explore and put out their ideas for analysis and feedback. Cynicism is based on distrust of the motives of others. Cynicism has contempt for accepted standards of how we behave. Having a cynical person in the room can quickly erode the sense of working together and seeing the possibilities. Cynicism is such an extremely difficult problem to overcome that many experts encourage organizations to never hire cynical people. They make group work almost impossible due to their comments not being based in logic, leaving no way to resolve their statements and move on.

The solution isn't always to just not invite cynics. Your meeting may include an expert on the topic that can't be replaced or support groups that have peripheral roles. You may be forced to invite an expert that happens to be the local negative cynic to get valuable information. You may be forced to invite a bystander who has a peevish perspective but eventually plays a downstream role.

These cynics bring their air of distrust and suspicious attitude along with them. Their continual flow of negativity through comments and non-verbals can reverse the ratio toward low performance.

As the lion tamer, be aware of the cynics in the room and refuse to let them get started. Question their assumptions and then request that the group move on. Laugh at humor, but do not allow sarcasm. Positive people often shut down with contempt if the cynic is allowed to be a bystander who is providing a continuous stream of negative, unfounded statements presented as facts, or sarcasm is creating an unsafe environment for discussion.

PLAY #10
THE RATIO OF CONNECTION: OTHER VS. SELF

The third ratio of communication that predicts high performance is the ratio of statements about yourself, your organization or your group to statements about others, other groups, and other organizations. The ratio of Other vs. Self statements is an indicator of personal connection.

Performance	Number of Statements	
	Other	Self
High	1	1.07
Medium	1	1.6
Low	1	29

The researchers observed 1 statement about Others for every 1.07 statements about Self in high performing organizations. The ratio was 1 Other statement for every 1.6 Self statements for medium performance, and 1 Other statement to every 29 Self statements for low performing companies. When the ratio of Other to Self was about the same, it predicted high performance. There were more statements about Self than Other in medium and low performing companies. In fact, low performing companies rarely talked about anything other than themselves.

A good rule of thumb is that there should be about one Other-focused statement for each Self-focused statement. There should be about the same amount of talking about yourself as talking about others. There should be about the same amount of talking about issues external to the group as those about issues internal to the group.

When the count of Other statements equals the count of Self statements, the end result is a better sense of who people and organizations are in relation to their environment. It is through finding out about others that a true picture of a person emerges, represented by their Self. It is the Math of the Extraordinary's Magic Ratio for understanding who you are in your world so you can create better connections with others.

Inquiry vs. Advocacy is about what do you want… vs. here's what I want… Other vs. Self is about who are you vs. here's who I am. Inquiry vs. Advocacy is about our position in problem-solving and decision-making. Other vs. Self is about building the bonds that create trust and establish how we are the same and how we are different. This ratio describes the attempts to create bonds of connection.

I have two personal stories that illustrate the deeply human connection that can be made or destroyed by the ratio of Other vs. Self.

THE AWARD & A MISSED OPPORTUNITY

As a young engineer, I had a good idea that turned out to be a great idea. In the early days of computer testing equipment, I automated a process that was tedious and required high-caliber machinists, electricians, and engineers to accomplish a precision calibration. My automated process was used multiple times almost every day and was more accurate, required fewer people, and took less time. The estimated one-time cost savings was over $1 million, with a projected $500,000 annual savings on an ongoing basis. What I did would be considered simple today. Actually, it would be a no-brainer, but at the time, the automated process combined several systems in a way no one in our environment had ever considered.

 This innovation with its large cost savings resulted in my receiving a corporate award. The organization where I worked had hundreds of engineers and technical professionals, plus an entire laboratory full of PhD's. Not only was my system award-winning, it was remarkable that a young engineer, especially a woman engineer, would win an award when our staff of scientists regularly received global recognition. So, it was a big deal for me.

The award came with a custom plaque and a $1000 cash prize. One Friday afternoon, my manager and I drove to a different site for a meeting with the VP of our division. I recall dressing out of character with makeup and a dress, and my boss had a fresh haircut and was wearing his three-piece suit. We wanted to look our best for this important event.

Eventually, we were escorted into the VP's office. His desk was piled high with papers and it seemed that we were keeping him from something much more important. Eventually, he leaned back in his chair and started talking. And he kept on talking. He talked for about half an hour. He told us about all the great things he had done as a young engineer. He told us of his accomplishments as a manager. He didn't ask me what I had done to achieve this award; he did not ask me about my innovative project; and he didn't ask my manager any questions either. He pontificated about himself. Finally, he stood up and dug out a large padded envelope and handed me my plaque and an envelope that contained the check. He and I shook hands, and my manager and I left.

Riding back to our office, I realized that I was frustrated. At the time, all I could think of was *And I dressed up for this!* I had worked hundreds of hours and created something important for my company, but the people in charge didn't seem to care what I had done or what I might be able to do next. To add insult to injury, when I looked at the check, it was not $1000 as promised. It was $739.28 because income tax had been taken out. When I left work that day, I went directly to the credit union and asked them to apply the check to my car note. I did not celebrate. I just went on with my life. Somehow getting a big award didn't seem like much after all.

For years afterward, I thought that perhaps I was being petty and didn't really understand my place in the scheme of things. Who was I to think an important man would care about something I had done? However, after studying the ratios of Extraordinary Performance, I now understand what happened that afternoon.

Our VP got this ratio all wrong. He had the opportunity to build a connection with a young person who might be the one to someday sit in his seat. He could have created a supporting voice at the lower level of the ranks to speak up positively when he announced new division programs. However, rather than starting a connection with me by offering some personal information about his career and then asking me about mine, his behavior subconsciously let me know that I did not matter. My frustration came from not being seen as evidenced by his apparent lack of interest in me or what I had accomplished. It would not have taken him any additional time. All he had to do was spend 1/3 of the time talking about himself, another third of the time learning about my project, and another third engaging with my boss. In fact, if the VP had let my boss and I join in the conversation, it would have been less effort for him. He got the ratio of Other vs. Self all wrong.

I TRUST YOU BECAUSE YOU ARE LIKE ME

I coached a young engineer named Clark who was a rising star in his corporation. He had spent 10 years in the ranks of research and development in a facility in the Northeast, and after a brief stint in manufacturing, was now the General Manager at a small facility in Alabama that was responsible for a few key components. The facility was located in a rural area over 50 miles from a medium-sized city. It was clear that his corporation had big plans for him by the variety of experiences he had been provided. But first, he needed to demonstrate that he could bring an organization together and create high-performance.

When I first met with Clark, he had been on the job for almost a year. His facility continued to have performance problems. Clark told me he couldn't get people to work with him. From his managers to the lowest ranking employees, Clark was isolated. He could not get them to engage at all with his ideas about improving their work and production numbers. I talked with Clark several times over the next few weeks, and it became clear to me that he was incredibly focused on the organization's tasks. Although he had good intentions, he believed that success would happen when people showed up, focused on their task, and got work done. In his way of thinking, there was no room for the daily banter that went on among the workforce. He was determined to set an example of hard work by arriving early, staying late, and being all business during the workday.

At this point, Clark was at his wit's end. He had no other ideas on how to engage with his workforce. I asked him to try two steps to changing the dynamic. I reminded him that his facility was located in an area of college football fanatics and that he had attended a Northern Division I school with its own proud football tradition. His first step would be to print off the upcoming fall football schedule for his school in color so that it would grab attention, then to put it under the glass on his desktop.

The second step was to let his employees know something about him. Clark and his two sons had floated down the Grand Canyon the summer prior to his accepting this position. I asked if he had any photos of the three of them in the Canyon and Clark beamed when he replied that he did. I asked him to put an 11x14 framed photo on the wall of the three of them on that adventure.

I admit that Clark left my office shaking his head that day. He had wanted to know the words to say or the memo to write to fix his problem. He didn't really see the use of my two steps, but promised to do them anyway. He was bankrupt and didn't have any better options.

I met with Clark again in about two months and began my conversation by asking him how the things we had talked about were working. He smiled and shook his head sheepishly, "Two days after the schedule was on my desk, one of my employees saw it and struck up a conversation about football. We probably talked for 15 minutes about the future of our teams for the upcoming season. Before it was over, he reminded me that the local high school football team was pretty good and most of the plant showed up on Friday nights to watch them. He invited me to come along."

"Then, a manager noticed the picture of me and my boys in the Grand Canyon. He looked at it closely and then asked if those were my boys. He said that they looked to be about the age of his boys, and asked where they went to school, stating that our kids might be classmates. Before I knew it my family and I were invited to local church events, football games, and even a few cookouts. Suddenly, my staff was talking and we are now working together."

Clark learned an important lesson about Other vs Self. It wasn't that Clark talked about himself; Clark didn't share enough about himself so that people had a sense of who he was and could connect with him. Once he offered a glimpse into who he was, his employees reached back toward him. He learned that Extraordinary Performance takes more than just executing the task. It also takes practicing the lessons provided by the communication ratios from the Math of the Extraordinary.

CREATING EXTRAORDINARY PERFORMANCE

INTRODUCTION

THE ROCKY FLATS STORY

I read a story of incredible performance. It was an account of the demolition of the Department of Energy's (DOE) Rocky Flats Plant and how it was transformed from an impossible mission of environmental remediation to a National Wildlife Refuge. It is a story of how a project that was estimated to take 70 years at a cost of $36 Billion was completed in 10 years at a cost of $6 Billion with significantly better quality than what was required.

The Rocky Flats Plant, located between Denver and Boulder, Colorado, was in operation from 1952 to 1992. The original site was 4 miles square, and was surrounded by seven different guard fences. Rocky Flats' mission was to manufacture the plutonium components of nuclear weapons. These parts had tight tolerances and difficult to manufacture features. The facility was known for meeting high quality standards and delivering on schedule.

However, in 1989, the FBI and EPA raided the plant based on informant's reports of unsafe conditions and illegal activities. The problem wasn't the manufactured parts – it was primarily because of the way environmental waste was handled. Eventually, legal action was initiated against the operating contractor and resulted in assessment of significant fines. Production was shut down permanently in 1992 and the mission became one of dismantling the facility and restoring the environment. The story of the downfall of Rocky Flats is one of intrigue and power. I encourage you to read it for yourself.

However, our story is one about success and Extraordinary Performance that started in 1995 when Kaiser-Hill took over the contract to dismantle and restore, and an impossible task was turned into a success. How did Kaiser-Hill bring about the culture change that created this Extraordinary Performance?

ELAINE'S SOURCES

The discipline of Positive Organizational Leadership is based on applying the findings in the field of positive psychology to organizations. As I began my study of this new discipline that described modern day success in a way that fit with my personal beliefs, I found two major research studies that seemed to be cornerstones. The results of one of these studies are the basis for the plays in the Math of Extraordinary. The second study analyzed the incredible performance that occurred in the environmental remediation of the Rocky Flats Plant. Kim Cameron's book *Making the Impossible Possible: Leading Extraordinary Performance: The Rocky Flats Story* provides the details of what happened through recounting the story of events and transcripts of interviews with management and other employees, and is the basis of this section on Creating Extraordinary Performance.

When I teach about how to achieve Extraordinary Performance, I use the Rocky Flats story to set the stage. I always have everyone's attention when I ask if they want similar performance in their organization. The stunning reduction of schedule from 70 years to 10 years plus the cost reduction from $36 Billion to $6 Billion is always an attention getter. No one ever has a personal example that is close enough to even mention.

In my heart, I always suspected that one day I would teach this story and someone would jump up in front of a group and criticize me. I figured their personal experience would insist that the reported research was a lie. I frequently teach in the shadow of the sister DOE weapons facilities at Oak Ridge, Tennessee, and I was confident that someone who had been displaced when remediation of Rocky Flats was completed might have relocated to Oak Ridge. It was quite possible that someone in my classes would have first-hand knowledge of what really went on at Rocky Flats and would have inside information that discredited what I was teaching.

But, the story was too compelling to quit using it. And, my information came from the publications of a respected researcher. One winter day, I was speaking to a community Leadership Development group about the Math of Extraordinary. I always started my presentation with a disclaimer that I was merely the messenger and all my information came from reputable publications. The crowd was thrilled at what they learned and several people talked with me for a long time afterward. I noticed one fellow standing back, and when the room had cleared he approached and said, "I'm that guy who worked at Rocky Flats."

I immediately replied, "So how much of my story is wrong?"

He told me, "None of it. In fact, it's even better than what you told."

I invited him to meet me for lunch so I could learn more, and he asked if he could bring some friends who were local and had also worked with him at Rocky Flats.

At lunch, one of the men immediately handed me a color copy of a book cover and said, "You need to read this book to find out what happened. I am the Allen referred to in the Acknowledgements. I spent my last year at Rocky Flats working with Dr. Cameron to make sure that this book accurately recorded what happened."

I looked at what he had handed me and smiled. The book was *Making the Impossible Possible*. I grinned and said, "I've read this book. In fact, this book is the very reason we are sitting here today. I want to know more from all of you." With that introduction, we embarked on a wonderful conversation.

I learned more insights about creating Extraordinary Performance over a lunch than all the books and articles I've read. The plays in this section are from the published documents about what happened in the clean-up and remediation of the Rocky Flats facility and my conversation with people who were actually a part of creating this true story of Extraordinary Performance. What they did was not a lucky once-in-a-lifetime happening. After Rocky Flats, they took their thinking to create the extraordinary in subsequent projects around the country. I believe what they told me can also help you.

THE REST OF THE STORY

When the Rocky Flats Plant opened in 1951, it was in a remote location. The facility provided high-tech jobs in an area that had been primarily farming. Classified work was conducted behind extreme security fences, and the people who worked there did so for their entire career. When their children entered the workforce, they often came to work at the plant alongside their parents and grandparents. It became a sheltered community of families living and working in the shadow of the Rocky Flats Plant. After the FBI raid in 1989, the facility continued to produce some limited weapons parts. However, with the end of the Cold War plus the existing environmental problems, all production at the Rocky Flats Plant was halted in 1992. It was clear that Rocky Flats no longer had a mission. A cost of $700 million per year to keep the facilities safe, secure, heated, and ventilated was a tremendous expense and provided incentive to demolish it. Thus, in 1995, the Kaiser-Hill Company contracted to manage the facility, dispose of the hazardous waste, and commence environmental remediation.

In 2005, the project was completed and the site was turned over to the U.S. Fish and Wildlife Service as the Rocky Flats National Wildlife Refuge.

The success of the Rocky Flats environmental remediation is based on understanding people and focusing on the real goal. It is a story of positive relationships and a willingness to see tasks differently. The following plays use examples from Dr. Cameron's research and from people who worked on the project. They have carried the key elements to other organizations. I am grateful for their willingness to reflect and share their lessons with me.

PLAY #11

THAT'S CRAZY. NO WAY.

The Kaiser-Hill Company was a joint venture that combined expertise with managing large construction projects, complex government facilities, and environmental remediation. Upon their arrival at the Rocky Flats site, the Kaiser-Hill team of more than 50 people seemed out of place. Rocky Flats was a nuclear weapons parts manufacturing facility with a history of solid performance that had also generated hazardous waste by-products. This team had no experience with weapons manufacturing and little in working with nuclear materials and their waste. The 7000 people on-site couldn't believe that such an inexperienced team was sent to manage such a dangerous and large task.

This disconnect between the plant's past history and the task at hand is exactly what enabled the Extraordinary Performance at Rocky Flats. When I asked "How were you able to toss out the estimate of $36 Billion and 70 years", my lunch mates laughed and said,

"We looked at this beat-up old set of buildings and said 'That's Crazy! Nothing costs this much. We've done plenty of big projects and nothing takes that much time and costs that much money.' We basically ignored all the studies that laid out the steps and estimated the cost. It didn't make sense to us."

Kaiser-Hill's employees were able to apply common sense. They were not buried in the past and the details of all the failed attempts to begin the clean-up. They did not know that the concrete walls of the building were thick enough to withstand a nuclear blast. They had not spent the last 6 years being swatted down by the regulators. At the time, the regulators did not have clear standards for this type of work, and there seemed to be a different interpretation applied to every submission. It felt like going in circles.

The workforce at Rocky Flats, the regulators, and the state and federal oversight personnel had a long history of being told *No* and *That's not right* to everything they had tried to do. This ambiguity when it came to expectations had resulted in an attitude of cynicism and distrust. Thus, the process plans were based on extreme cases when creating cost estimates and schedules. When no visible progress toward remediation had occurred in six years, those involved with the project had no reason to believe progress would ever come, and certainly not come easily.

THE PLAY

There are two important lessons to take away from this play. When you are in the middle of something you know well – your discipline, your organization and your daily routine -- it is almost impossible to grasp a new perspective. Most likely, you can't even articulate all the assumptions that bind you to continuing the same old thing. All of the rules that go with what has become normal blind you to what might be. It's as if you are wearing blinders. Two questions that can help you think differently are:

- Does this make sense?
- If anyone else was doing this thing, would I think they were crazy and were not thinking clearly?

At Rocky Flats, the craziness went from top to bottom. Dr. Cameron recounts a story from an interview with a manager that illustrates how convoluted our thinking can become...and we actually believe it makes sense.

One of the first things we came up against in wanting to take down these guard posts was rules. [*One employee*], who worked for Kaiser-Hill, came to work and said,
"You told us to take down the guard post, but I can't take it down."
I said, "Why not?"
"Because the regulations require that before you take down a federal building, a public building, you must first offer it to the homeless."
I said, "Wait a minute, we're inside a protected area. There are signs on this building saying Danger Radiation. And before you can tear it down, we have to get some ruling from somebody that we've offered it to the public? That's crazy.
Get a bulldozer and knock it down. I'll take the flak."
And he went and got a bulldozer and knocked it down.
(example quoted from *Making the Impossible Possible*, Chapter 5, Symbolic Leadership Activities section)

It is almost impossible to hear your internal voice voice that says, "THIS IS CRAZY" when all the cues look the same as a past scenario. You can't see that your focus is on the wrong details and become trapped in your past.
One summer, I was teaching managers from a large organization at their facility. The plant site covered miles and had hundreds of old buildings.

When I walked into the classroom that morning, I knew something was wrong. Not only was the temperature in the room above 85, the humidity made the air thick. My students came in and we toughed it out for the first hour, but I realized that no one was learning. Instead, we were all busy wiping sweat and becoming more irritated by the minute. At the first break, the building manager let us know that maintenance had looked at the air-conditioning unit and found bad bearings. Unfortunately, there were no sets of bearings in the maintenance stores and it would be about two weeks before the air conditioning was repaired.

My class groaned and settled in to just tough it out. That was what their organization does in situations like this. They must follow purchasing regulations and get in line for maintenance service. However, I didn't work for this organization and my view was that it was crazy for us to waste the next two days going through the motions, but not learning anything due to the hot classroom. I had traveled a thousand miles to deliver an important message and felt an obligation to make the most of everyone's time. It was our chance to learn and I wasn't about to let it pass.

A supervisor from maintenance was in the class and I asked him if there was a bearing supplier in the city. I suggested that if he could find out if the supplier had bearings on hand and if it wasn't cost prohibitive, I would go purchase the bearings and they would magically appear next to the air-conditioning unit. It meant that much to me. The class looked at me as if I was the crazy one. I asked how many of them would want to share the cost. Their eyes became even wider. I reminded them that this was their one opportunity to work with me and I guaranteed that they would get their money's worth if we could get our problem fixed.

I then asked, "Surely somewhere on this huge facility there is a meeting room we can use for the next two days. Maybe we can use one today and another tomorrow. What are all our options?" The emotion in the room shifted from victim to enabled. Two people jumped up to make phone calls and in an hour we had relocated to a nice, cool room and were back in business.

They had been trained to put up with the system. I have worked in jobs where I was programmed to put up with the system. But, now, my goal when teaching is to do whatever is necessary for my students to learn. When there is a barrier to learning, I quickly get in *How else can we do this?* mode and try something different.

My general purpose signal that something simple is being treated with much more difficulty than it deserves is when I am amazed at the craziness of what we are willing to tolerate.

STEP 1: Pay attention to your internal voice that says, "That's crazy!"

STEP 2: Ignore any talk about obstacles and why things can't or won't work. These voices are the programming from normal behavior that are desperately trying to get you to stick with the usual.

STEP 3: Generate options by asking *How can we?* and *Does the resistance make sense or is it a rule from the past that doesn't fit now?*

PLAY #12

SETTING THE STAGE

My favorite story from *Making the Impossible Possible* about the successful clean-up and remediation of the Rocky Flats Plant seemed like a fairy tale. I told it relentlessly to my students because it was so compelling and irresistible to me. This example put together what I knew in my heart from personal experience but had not put into words and a formula. The story was an example of the research about how people work put into practice. It is the story of before and after, art and science, and emotion and facts. Over my lunch with the men who had worked on the project, I met the person behind the story and learned my favorite story was not a fairy tale. It was true.

When Kaiser-Hill took over the operating contract for the operation and remediation of the Rocky Flats Plant, things were at a standstill. There had been little real motion toward remediation. Study after study had been done to provide action plans, steps, schedules, and costs, with no resulting action. An agreement made yesterday with the federal and local environmental regulators would be invalid the next. But, imagine if you had been associated with the site for years. Or perhaps you had grown up in the shadow of the entity responsible for providing good jobs for your community and supporting your family, likely for more than a generation. What if your organization's history was one of manufacturing quality precision parts and delivering on schedule? It would be hard to imagine a huge facility of hundreds of buildings on 4 square miles simply not mattering anymore. It was nearly impossible to imagine the buildings and work at the Rocky Flats Plant disappearing and the prairie grass of the Front Range growing in its place.

When the FBI raided the facility in 1989, urban folklore raged about environmental abuses as a result of a federal indictment. Eventually, all of the allegations in the indictment were disproven, but the damage was done. People had heard and read about a horror story and that story has lingered on as it took years in the courts to reach resolution. In fact, one of the attorneys on the Justice Department's investigative team testified before Congress that, "Virtually none of the allegations contained in the search warrant were borne out after a full investigation."

What if you were a regulator and had witnessed years of arguments about handling environmental waste and then the raid by the FBI because of alleged illegal activities? Would you believe that nothing had really been going on? Would you believe decontamination and clean-up activities would truly change, and contractors could be trusted to do the right thing?

In 1995, when Kaiser-Hill arrived at Rocky Flats, everyone seemed at odds with opposing views resulting in angry disagreements. There were protests and protesters. Community meetings to discuss the project resulted in near brawls. The federal managers and contractor management had difficulty agreeing on what should be done and the order in which to do it. The workforce resisted activities to dismantle the equipment and begin clean-up.

Then a simple action brought about an incredible turn of events. One of Kaiser-Hill's VP's had the idea that a *Before and After* representation of the site would help people understand the clean-up mission. Per Kaiser-Hill's design plan, a local graphic design company modified an aerial photo of the current plant to show what the Rocky Flats site would look like when the work was complete. A crude photorealistic image was created that put green blocks in place of the plant and its roads, buildings, guard towers, and fences to create a *Before and After* visual image.

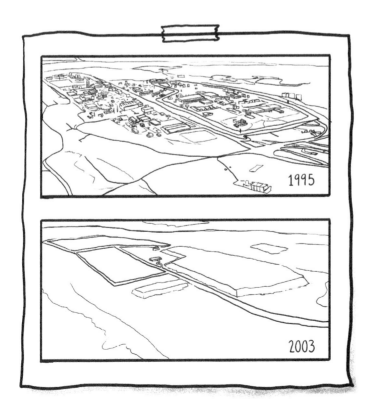

One of these photo-realistic posters of *Before and After* was propped up on an easel in a public meeting room at the plant site. A photographer from the local newspaper in Boulder, the Daily Camera, happened to be at a public meeting and took a photo of the poster. The next Sunday, his picture of the *Before and After* poster was on the front page with the caption, *Is This How Rocky Flats Will Appear?*

Suddenly, with one look, everyone suddenly understood, "Oh, that's what we are doing!" This serendipitous event ignited a widespread change in perspective by community groups, federal and local regulators and, most importantly, the workforce. The project and the end state of returning the site to its original prairie suddenly seemed real. Management and workers at the plant, federal and local oversight participants, and the local community started pulling together to make this project happen.

WHAT HAPPENED

How could such a simple thing as a poster with a crude rendition of the *After* visual image of the site make such a difference? It *Set the Stage.* The explanation lies in understanding how the brain works. For details on the topic of how the brain works, and more about creating images that move people, see the play *Tell the Story.* The details about brain functioning are in the Introduction of the section on Harnessing Your Horsepower.

I had a chicken or egg problem in preparing this part of the book. I wanted to talk about how to create performance, but I also needed for the reader to understand how people work. I started with creating.

Think of our cognitive abilities as having two parts. One part (we will call it Right Brain) focuses on the big picture, sees patterns, and puts details together in new ways to create something new. This part doesn't have verbal skills and hangs out in the background. The other part (we will call it Left Brain) focuses on step-by-step actions and time. It is also dominant and focused on execution.

The plans, steps, cost, and schedule are all favorite activities of Left Brain, and since Left Brain is dominant, we often jump right into creating steps and goals before we get the picture. Unfortunately, starting with a list of steps doesn't create a picture. It takes seeing a picture first and then creating the steps that build on each other to create the desired results.

At Rocky Flats, the work being done was met with resistance until everyone had the picture in mind that, at the end, there would be a prairie in place of

SETTING THE STAGE   123

buildings. Until the stage was set, if a machine was being disassembled, it was done in a way that it could be put back together because surely it might be needed again. It is incredibly difficult to get funding for new buildings, so resistance to tearing down perfectly good structures was high. People most likely didn't know why they were resisting – they just knew that this new direction did not fit into their personal mental vision of Rocky Flats.

Once people saw the visual image of the restored Front Range prairie, work commenced and accelerated. They internalized that disassembling and decontaminating a machine meant to clean it up, pack it in a box, and ship it out. The thinking such as we should scavenge spare parts from this machine in case we need it for one of the remaining machines changed because the crew suddenly had their internal perspective altered. They internalized that the all the machines would be leaving, and there was no need for parts for the future.

Other synergies started once everyone got the picture. Suddenly, agreements were made to transport the hazardous waste across the country to permanent storage facilities. All of the concerns about *why it should be done* changed to *how are we going to do it.*

The obstacles that were being thrown up in an unconscious attempt to keep life the same disappeared when everyone could see themselves in the picture of the future.

SETTING THE STAGE

Since *Setting the Stage* with a vision of the end state is so important, why doesn't it happen? The answer is simple, but knowing the cause doesn't make *Setting the Stage* popular or necessarily easy. In fact, the only way to be willing to Set the Stage is to understand its importance and embrace the resistance you will meet. It seems like a waste of time and resources to most people, who in true Left Brain mode, want to get on with the action.

The reason we don't Set the Stage is that it takes time and has no obvious tie to the bottom line. Left Brain is in charge and sees storytelling and pictures on the wall as a waste. Left Brain values steps, details, costs and schedules. Left Brain believes that if you lay out the action plan with attached cost and schedule, all it takes is execution to be successful. And, since Left Brain is in charge, this regimented course of definite action prevails.

What Left Brain can't see is that no plan of action can ever be complete enough to bring everyone to the same end point. There is always interpretation, and without the end imagery, every step is interpreted in a way to meet each individual's personal end picture.

Those who are inspired become committed to a task. Inspiration creates emotional energy. When groups accomplish Extraordinary Performance, it takes more than the prescribed steps. As projects unfold and someone recognizes a gap or obstacle that was unforeseen, the imagery guides them to figure out how to jump the crevasse or remove the obstacle so that the picture happens. And, typically, it is not only one someone. Every day, in every task, the players figure out how to make it work because they can envision the result.

Setting the Stage can be an actual picture. It can be a story. For example, you might take your team on a field trip to see your vision actually working at another facility. Seeing the pieces individually isn't enough. It takes a vision, image, a story or a real life setting for everyone to understand where they are going and what it will look like when they get there.

IKEA is a master of *Setting the Stage*. IKEA is a provider of home goods, furniture, kitchen utensils, kitchen cabinets, and anything you could ever need for your house or apartment. There are lots of things to learn at an IKEA store. When you visit an IKEA store, they have their merchandise on display in groupings. You can walk through a section of sofas, beds, lamps and other home goods grouping. However, around the outside of the store are actual rooms that have their products staged so you can see how they go together. They even have entire small apartments setup so you can see how to get your life neatly arranged in a few hundred square feet. People often talk about buying a room design from IKEA, and they can easily purchase it and walk out the door. They see the end state. They can sit in their new bedroom, kitchen or living room to see how it feels. The vision is clear.

Setting the Stage takes time. It requires people to stop their preference of doing activities to meet goals rather than first listening to a story and grasping the vision. Stories and images appear to have no value added because there is not a direct tie to the bottom line. There is no marker in the schedule of activities that gets a box checked for hearing a story, seeing a picture, or taking a field trip. However, it is the foundation for achieving your goals and the harness that gets everyone pulling together.

PLAY #13

ALIGNING PERSPECTIVES

Nothing seemed to be happening quickly at Rocky Flats. In 1995, after years of working toward cleaning the place up, over $60 million in incentive fees had been paid and lots of studies had been done. But, there were more people on the payroll every year and nothing was moving out the gate to permanent storage or to the trash heap. Insiders predicted that the 70 year, $36 Billion estimate was not even close to what it would take to complete the job. Many people believed the Rocky Flats Plant would never be reduced to a memory.

It was easy to believe that this job would take generations to complete. For instance, there were over 1000 gloveboxes in the facility. A glovebox is exactly what is implies: A box with gloves that a person uses to handle whatever is in the box.

Gloveboxes were used to protect unusual materials from the environment and to protect people from the material. Plutonium is an extremely hazardous material, and much of the work done on it was performed with a custom designed glovebox enclosing the part. Although they sound simple, gloveboxes at facilities such as Rocky Flats are incredibly complicated and expensive. They come in all sizes and some can extend for a long distance to contain a part through many different processes. Parts are moved along from station to station by rolling tables or by hoists.

Once all work to produce parts had ceased at Rocky Flats, the highly skilled machinists began disassembling their old manufacturing process and machines. It typically took a year to dismantle and ship out a glovebox. With over 1000 of them, it was easy to believe that dismantling the whole facility would take a very long time.

However, one day someone realized that they didn't have to take the gloveboxes apart down to every bolt the way machinists do things. The equipment was headed for the scrap pile, never to be used again in its current form. Once the machinists realized that all they had to do was decontaminate the equipment and then get it into pieces that would fit on the waste truck, the work became rough construction instead of precision manufacturing. They reduced the time of clean-up and clear-out from one glovebox per year to days or weeks, depending on the size and complexity of the equipment.

Process improvements such as this incredible improvement in accomplishing glovebox demolition are often attributed to a can-do attitude and a willingness to accept ideas and innovation. My lunch-mates explained the change in a different way. Their view on what really happened is a key factor to helping change happen, and is a theme that started with the play *That's Crazy. No Way.* It's a matter of your viewpoint that determines your course of action. The Kaiser-Hill management team had a history of big projects dealing with waste and construction, and they didn't see the project as being nearly as big or as complex as those who viewed it with their manufacturing operations perspective and background. They didn't see the project as a take-apart and packaging-for-storage task. They saw it as a clean-up and dispense-of project.

The workforce tearing down the plant was made up of the same workers who had world-class skills for making precision parts from difficult materials. They had expertise in attending to tedious details to achieve part tolerances. The engineers and technicians had years of experience designing complex systems with tight tolerances, precision instrumentation, and complex chemical reactions. So, when this group of dedicated people went to their new roles in demolishing the plant, they took along their same perspective about doing this work as when they were making high-tech parts.

The problem was that rough demolition work was being done with the same loving care demanded by their past tasks. Disassembling a glovebox to a machinist or engineer accustomed to careful attention to every detail meant that each bolt was removed and packed away. Each piece was removed. They were taking the gloveboxes apart as if someday they would have the task of putting them back together.

My lunch companions described another example of how the workforce unknowingly applied their perspective of keeping the plant running to tearing it down in a way that slowed progress. There was a warehouse-type building which housed large tanks that held hazardous chemicals. These tanks were sturdy and designed to withstand harsh conditions and rough handling. The demolition process required that each tank be drained, and then the tank would be disposed of. When the facility was operating, removal of a tank meant cleaning it up and then cutting it into pieces small enough to be moved through the building's door. After being cut into a smaller size, the tank pieces were then put in boxes for shipment. This same process was being used in this final demolition of the indoor tank farm.

I'm sure you know the solution by now. But, it was an epiphany when the realization came that the building was to be torn down anyway, so why not knock a big hole in the wall and, once they were drained, simply bring the tanks directly to the truck. Why add on extra work to cut the tanks to sizes that could fit through the door and add on the labor of building and packing boxes? There was no sense in working around obstacles in the building in order to avoid damaging a structure that was coming down anyway.

All of these solutions seem obvious in hindsight. The lesson from these events is not the actual solutions. One of the barriers to demolishing the plant was that people who were trained in creating and maintaining a world-class manufacturing facility were asked to apply their thinking and creating skills to tearing down. They were doing clean-up and demolition work the same way they made parts; exactly and with great precision.

The lesson is to *Align Perspectives*. Aligning Perspectives means that the person doing the work applies their base skills to the nature of the task. It means that who you think you are is aligned with the nature of the task. We assume this happens automatically, but most of us grab up our favorite tools to attack whatever problem is put before us. We jump right in, especially when the cues look familiar. We forget to watch how people that do this sort of task all the time do it because we think we know the task.

The machinists at Rocky Flats still needed to think about how things went together and use their hands to work with equipment and tools. However, they needed to be smart about the fastest way to take things apart instead of the most accurate way to make parts. Riggers and millwrights at the tank farm needed to think about the most efficient way to take an entire process and it's building apart instead being constrained by the overhead door opening of a building soon to be demolished.

Progress at Rocky Flats accelerated once the workforce internalized that they were no longer working in manufacturing. They were at a construction site, and every month success would be measured by how much of the site was gone and by how many people had worked themselves out of a job. The workforce's vision of the mission at the Rocky Flats Plant was turned completely around by aligning their perspective with the task.

PLAY #14

THE SWEET SPOT

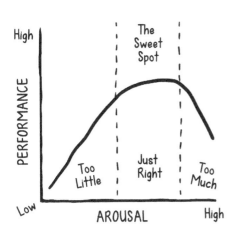

In the discipline of Sport Psychology, one of our goals is to help athletes consistently reach the Sweet Spot of performance. The mental side of performance depends on arousal – the extent to which an individual is energized. The Sweet Spot is how we refer to a mental state where performance is at its best. In 1908, psychologists Robert Yerkes and John Dodson conducted a famous experiment that has become a building block of how we think about creating consistent high performance. The Yerkes-Dodson law explains that too little arousal creates poor performance, and too much arousal also creates poor performance. In the middle is just the right amount of arousal to create the sweet spot for best performance.

They discovered this principle when experimenting with mice doing a task. A little shock didn't seem to motivate the mice to do the task. Then, an increased shock level increased performance on the task. However, at a further point of increasing the shock, the mice quit and performance dropped. Their conclusion was that a little excitement was not enough, too much excitement became stress and was too much, but in the middle, there was a sweet spot of just enough.

In a more modern-day study, college males were falsely told that the ability to throw a tennis ball at a 12-inch target about 20 feet away was an important indicator of success in sports that involve throwing. These wanna-be athletes were determined to do their best to show their athletic ability by their performance on this supposedly key indicator. After 10 practice throws:

- Some participants were told that 90% of their peers performed better than they did, implying that they were in the bottom 10% on this key indicator of an athletic skill. This feedback, even though it was false, was intended to create high arousal or a stressful situation because the participants believed they were in a category of not having the natural ability from the results of their practice attempts. They were led to believe that they really needed to try harder to even be at an acceptable level of performance.

- Another group was told that only 30% of peers did better than they did to create a sense of being good enough resulting in low arousal. This group felt they didn't have anything to worry about because they were naturally in the group of high performers.
- The third group was led to believe that they were about at the middle of the pack by being told 60% of their peers performed better to create a sweet spot of arousal. These participants knew they could be successful because they were already doing well. They focused to try to do even better.

Then the participants were allowed to make a second set of throws for what they believed was an evaluation of their potential as athletes in tasks that involved throwing. Just as the Yerkes-Dodson Law predicted, those thinking they were already good enough (low arousal) had poor scores, those with high arousal tightened up from the stress of not being good enough and had median scores, but those in the middle had the best scores. Too much pressure to perform creates poor performance, just like too little energy results in lackluster execution.

The simple explanation is that we don't focus when we think we have a task mastered and we tighten up out of fear of failure when we are overly stressed. This explanation works for sporting events and in everyday life. However, when our reaction to events is *not enough* or *too much* it becomes impossible to create the extraordinary.

The problem with too much or too little arousal is the effect on our ability to recognize and process cues. When people are in a state of low arousal and not adequately energetic, they see plenty of cues, but don't do a very good job of picking out what matters so they can act on it. They can see the forest, but can't see the individual trees, the two paths ahead, or the grizzly bear sitting in the middle of one path. They focus on information that doesn't really matter and don't recognize what is important. Thus they make wrong moves and poor decisions. They don't react in the best way, and often seem to be a step behind.

On the other hand, when people are in a state of high arousal, there is a lot of energy, but it isn't focused on the right things. People who are overly anxious restrict what they choose to act on, and miss relevant cues and information. They don't appear to be in slow motion, but they seem to be making missteps, usually because they have narrowed their focus to the wrong things. They often pick up too many cues and can't figure out what they should do. Their fear of not doing well causes hesitation and over-thinking. They tighten up and become fearful of possible bad results. These people see the forest, the trees, the paths, the grizzly bear, the flowers along the path, and start wondering why the bear isn't in hibernation since it is still early March! They miss out that self-preservation should be their focus.

When people have the moderate energy of the Sweet Spot, they use fewer cues, but pick out the more relevant ones. They start to see what is important. They understand what matters. They can filter out the irrelevant information and more clearly recognize the important info. They make better decisions and take appropriate action because they are working with the best data. They see the forest, the trees, the options of two paths and can choose the path without the grizzly bear. They are better at identifying what matters and discarding the irrelevant distractions.

NO MORE BURNING PLATFORMS

Books and courses on implementing change are plagued with a cliché. A crucial part of motivating people to move from one place to another is creating a sense of urgency. Change experts insist that people believe they have no choice in the matter. People must be convinced that if they stay where they are, the business collapses, relationships fail, and disaster looms.

Unfortunately, this sense of urgency is usually presented as a Burning Platform. Attempts to get action are based on threats and fear. The Burning Platform is based on a visual where you are on a platform that is on fire. If you stay where you are, you'll go up in flames with the old ways. As scary as it is to jump to something new, staying behind will result in sure disaster. The visual of the platform on fire is so powerful with its all-or-nothing outcome, action-oriented managers can't resist pushing for progress using this cliché.

No doubt, creating a sense of urgency is crucial. Doing it with the threat of a burning platform simply doesn't work. The Burning Platform creates negative emotions of anxiety, uncertainty, and stress. The Extraordinary Performance that is a key element of change demands that people be in the Sweet Spot mental state of curiosity, excitement, and collaboration. The Burning Platform doesn't inspire; instead, it puts people in a state of arousal where performance deteriorates. People respond with either low arousal

where they know it is hopeless and don't try or high arousal where they miss important information even though they are trying really hard. As new processes are being developed, increasing pressure to the point of do or die creates a state where focus becomes narrowed and other important cues are missed. At the very time people need to be noticing and sorting through information, they put on their blinders or smoky-grey glasses. They can't see clearly.

Many years ago, I worked in an organization which depended on getting new business for us to stay in business. A major part of my role was getting new clients. Unfortunately, I am not a superstar when it comes to business development. In fact, I would starve if my profession was sales. With a downturn in the economy, I had grown more concerned each day about whether my projects would secure enough funding for me to keep my job. One afternoon my boss summoned me to his office to discuss prospects for the upcoming year. I was frank about the poor prospects. Upon hearing my projections, he said, "You know that if you don't find more funding for your project, you don't have a job."

His response was intended to create a Burning Platform that would fire me up to find funding. The reality of not having employment created so much stress, I spent the next two months marginally doing my job because I was focused on applying for different positions and going on job interviews.

Burning Platforms can cause people to jump, but they might not jump where you want them to jump. They may jump in the water, work harder to put out the fire, or hunker down, depressed about their upcoming incineration.

There is a new reason to avoid threatening with a Burning Platform in an attempt to create urgency. In mid-2015, the demographic of the workplace changed. There are now more of the Millennial generation and younger generations than the combination of Baby Boomers and Gen-X'ers. (Baby Boomers are those born before 1964; Gen-X'ers were born 1965-1977; Gen-Y (Millennials) were born 1978-1991; Gen-Z were born 1991-2002) The older segment of the workforce has a preference for loyalty to a company and will tolerate ups and downs without leaving. This growing younger segment of the workforce actually plans on leaving for greener pastures. For this younger group, I teach that if they stay with a company for a long time, they have decided many, many times that maybe they will hang around a little longer for a specific reason. Providing a Burning Platform will give them an excuse to jump because they were planning on leaving anyway. They are more likely to stay to be part of a new, improved vision with new opportunities. Their response to a threat will be to move on to a place with potential instead of staying around to go up in flames.

Threats aren't positive and they push people out of *The Sweet Spot*. Creating a Burning Platform is a threat.

THE SWEET SPOT OF URGENCY

Arousal is alertness, excitement, and being energized. The Sweet Spot for Extraordinary Performance is created by an urgency and excitement about reaching the future state. There is a new goal and people want to get there. They see a brighter future. They see possibilities from a new recognition of relevant cues and have the ability to discard what doesn't really matter. There is progress toward something better.

Sarcasm and Cynicism cast a dark cloud over urgency by distorting reality and creating distrust of possibilities. A list of steps, complete with cost and schedule, is often used in an attempt to prove the future state. While the steps are critical for making progress and organizing, the story and vision of what's to come is what ignites excitement and turns on optimal performance.

A key skill for getting people in the Sweet Spot is telling the story of what life will look like after the change. A sense of urgency comes from excitement about getting to the better place. When the vision of a better life is internalized, people start asking *Why wait? Let's go now*. Without the vision of the future state, people are uncertain about whether the change is even valid and how they fit in. Then with either too much or too little excitement and anxiety, they start missing the important cues. The play *Setting the Stage* discusses the importance of providing a story illustrating the end result and provides ideas for how to create and tell stories.

A PERSONAL LANDING PAD

Another key skill for keeping people in *The Sweet Spot* is removing uncertainty and ambiguity. Uncertainty and ambiguity are dark clouds that suck the very life out of a desire to change – even for something better. Over lunch with the men who had worked at Rocky Flats, I asked the question, "How did you convince people to tear down the facility that had paid their family's bills for generations, and do it at record speed? How did you inspire people to work themselves out of a job as fast as they could?"

Their response was what I call a Personal Landing Pad. In the Rocky Flats project, everyone from the lowest ranking to the highest ranking person had a written plan of where they would be on the Monday after their job disappeared. A worker might participate in tearing down their own building one week, literally working themselves out of a job, but they didn't have a fear of their job being over and wondering what was next. Every worker, both blue collar and white collar, had a written and approved plan of where they would land. About 6000 people needed to be absorbed in the Boulder/Denver area over the 10-year period of the project and, with state and local planning, each person knew what would be happening for them. The Rocky Flats employees knew what was next. The Kaiser-Hill professionals knew where their next project would be. No one had any hesitation about the future because they knew what it would look like. Uncertainty was banished.

My lunch-mates shook their heads as they remembered their own written plans of what would happen after their work ended at Rocky Flats. These were professionals who would readily be able to find new work and most likely move to new positions in their current company. They talked about how difficult it was for them to create their own personal plan for leaving even though they came to the site knowing it was temporary. These were people who had arrived in 1995 specifically to take down the plant and then move on. It must have been almost impossible for the people who had lived and worked their entire lives at Rocky Flats to envision a different future. As easy as it sounds to create a landing pad, it is emotionally charged and takes trust in those that are making promises about the next step.

It was important to keep the workforce in the Sweet Spot to achieve Extraordinary Performance. There was a financial reward for moving fast into the future. Kaiser-Hill's contract with the Department of Energy included penalties for late completion and bonuses for every day the project was completed ahead of schedule. There was a set payout schedule for splitting up a percentage of the bonuses to reward the workers for getting to the finish line ahead of schedule.

With the combination of bonuses and the landing pads, the motivation for Extraordinary Performance became a race to the finish line instead of the threat of a Burning Platform.

Getting people in the Sweet Spot uses a combination of plays and skills. The steps to the Sweet Spot for Extraordinary Performance are:

STEP 1: From the Plays *Setting the Stage* and *Tell the Story*, develop a story, picture, or vision of what life will look like in the new state. Pictures and illustrations speak directly to people so they can understand what is happening. This understanding is the preface to execution and implementation. To generate your story or picture, close your eyes and imagine yourself in the new environment. What does it look like? What do you do in the new environment? How do you interact with other people? This story must be literal – a tale of percentage increases and projected facts is not adequate because it does not speak to Right Brain. You need to provide a description of the future that speaks to the five senses instead of using percentages, charts and numbers. The most difficult part of getting an actual picture is that you'll need to really understand the change plus find the funds for an illustrator!

STEP 2: Insist on each person having their own landing pad. Develop a format and a system for each person to have a written scenario of what they will be doing the day their current position is eliminated or changes are made to the new system. This landing pad includes schedules, tasks, pay, and benefits; and must be approved by management. Creating these plans for each and every person requires coordination between different groups as they vie for the same spots. It also requires a clear vision of the opportunities and changes in current roles. You can expect resistance from managers who don't believe in the future state, and from those who deflect possibilities with cynical distrust of the motives of those leading the change.

STEP 3: Identify those who see possibilities and also use the ratios from the Math of the Extraordinary to keep people engaged.

STEP 4: Watch carefully for those who damage enthusiasm with sarcasm and cynicism. Negativity pushes arousal into the too little and too much ends of the Inverted-U diagram. Distrust and uncertainty causes some people to become even more anxious and more aroused, while it causes some people to shut down. Either way, at the too much or too little ends of the arousal scale, performance goes down.

PLAY #15

OBSTACLES TO EXTRAORDINARY PERFORMANCE

ELAINE: What happened next in your career after Rocky Flats?
THEY SMILED AND SAID: We moved on to other Department of Energy sites that needed environmental remediation. Environmental restoration has become our expertise and we move from site to site. Those of us from Rocky Flats are spread all over the world now. We have been many other places and now are at this location to work on remediation projects here with different companies.
ELAINE: The story of Rocky Flats is incredible. Were you able to take your strategies of how to create such extraordinary performance to other places with the same results? Or, was Rocky Flats just a lucky fluke?

At this point, the smiles toned down and their heads nodded maybe. These players at Rocky Flats worked for different companies now and the government participants had moved on to other positions. Times had changed. However, my new friends believed some key levers that had enabled the Extraordinary Performance at Rocky Flats had been lost. With hindsight, they could see the changes. It was clear that this was not the first time my new-found friends had discussed why things were different.

Their insights on why it has been difficult to duplicate the Extraordinary Performance seen at Rocky Flats describe obstacles we face every day. The first obstacle lies in our reluctance to believe what we cannot measure. The second obstacle comes from trying to serve two masters.

YOU GOTTA' BELIEVE

At Rocky Flats, they celebrated. They had a party when the first shipment of material left the site. Each year, they rented a ballroom in the Boulder-Denver area for a site-wide Christmas party for the employees and their families, complete with Santa and gifts for everyone. They worked together, played together, and celebrated their successes from small to large. Kaiser-Hill managers had large budgets to keep the positive energy going from the recognition of progress. My lunch-mates talked about relationships they made during their years on the project and how they still kept up with their friends. Kaiser-Hill knew that celebration was expensive, but they also could see that they were starting to be under the budget and ahead of schedule. Good things were happening with a potentially resistant workforce. Union grievances were reduced from 900 per year in 1994 to a handful. People expecting life-long employment were working themselves out of a job as fast as they could.

Kaiser-Hill had also pledged to return 20% of their profits to their employees as bonuses. As profits grew, so did the bonus pool. Each employee's bonus was calculated depending on position and time on the job as a part of the overall profit. Twenty percent seemed like an extreme amount to return to the workers, but the bonus was growing daily as the work was completed at a faster rate and at less cost. More than 200 technological innovations from new ideas and ways of thinking were embraced as they improved safety and faster performance...and grew the bonus.

There is absolutely no hard connection between dollars spent on celebrations and overall profit. That's the problem with creating synergy. There is no research that provides tabular data of recommended celebration hours and bonus dollars per employee to achieve Extraordinary Performance. For instance, when it comes to justifying these types of funds, it is hard to compete for financial resources against a new machine that has a readily calculated ROI based on time, labor, or material savings versus spending money on something that doesn't have a tangible return on investment.

The problem starts when organizations disassemble their financial costs into specific categories in a search for places to cut or reduce funds. It is faulty thinking that every expenditure has a clear tie to the bottom line. However, since computers keep up with that sort of information, it is easy to get duped into thinking a line-by-line analysis of expenditures can reveal waste. It is a mistake to believe that the amount of expenditure for a perceived frivolous activity will improve the bottom line by that amount if those activities are removed. Cancelling the company softball league, firing the recreation coordinator, and selling the company park doesn't add those funds to the bottom line. In fact, it may be impossible to ever find those returned funds in the big picture as the synergistic relationships required for remarkable performance never happen. Most likely, cutting the opportunity for people to make connections will eventually damage the bottom line. Unfortunately, just like you can't prove the contribution of celebrations and bonus percentages, you can't find the loss in the math of the financial accounts either.

My lunch-mates told me that the hardest part of transferring what they learned at Rocky Flats was convincing their new companies to keep substantial party budgets and to maintain a 20% bonus plan. They talked about how upper management continually applied pressure to cut those funds so they could be converted directly to the profit reporting for the investors. Since there is no direct connection from the money spent on parties, it can seem frivolous and wasteful. The argument about bonuses originates in thinking about the purpose of the corporation. The purpose is to make money for the investors, and the bonus money is an obvious place to recoup more bottom line profit. Shouldn't as much of the profits as possible be returned to the investors? Plus, the workers signed up for their salary and are being paid well. Do you think anyone will really quit because the Christmas party was cancelled and the bonus pool was reduced from 15% to 13%?

For almost 20 years, the Great Place to Work® Institute has listed the top 100 Great Places to Work for each year. These companies out-perform their peers in the market consistently with better retention. Employees trust their leadership, take pride in their work, and have positive relationships with their fellow workers. The companies on the list, without exception, view a positive employee workplace experience as a non-negotiable component of their success. An analysis of employee interviews at these companies reads like a journal of life at Rocky Flats as they were in the midst of Extraordinary Performance. When you read the detailed reports of each company, it is clear that employees like to go to work, they feel valued, and there is an unexplained synergy.

It's not the party that matters. It is the connections that are created when people are facilitated to meet each other's families. It's the relationships formed over a company-sponsored lunch by sharing a joke or dreams. It's the audience laughing together at the VP dancing with joy over meeting a milestone. It's the relationship that allows for disagreement without damage, simply because you know the other person and give them the benefit of doubt and are willing to listen respectfully.

The bonus arrangement with the workforce matters. The reward for extra effort to meet a goal matters. The recognition with a significant reward that lets employees know that the company depends on them beyond just a basic skill set creates synergy that crosses silos and boundaries.

It matters that company leaders do what they say they will do by holding to what they promised. One way to deal with cynicism is to not hire cynics. However, when the organization doesn't keep promises, they are growing their own internal cynics. These small changes that take away from the employee experience to benefit the organizational goals chip away at trust and turn employee performance into a commodity that suggests individuals don't matter. It starts the relationship killer of contempt.

Parties, celebrations, and bonuses are easy targets in attempts for companies to be more profitable. Unfortunately, as these disappear, so does the synergy that is the invisible force in Exceptional Performance.

BONUSES AND PERFORMANCE

In 1995, DOE and the Kaiser-Hill Company signed a contract for 5-years and $3.5 billion to manage the cleanup of the Rocky Flats Plant. They signed another contract at the conclusion of the first 5 years to finish the project. Kaiser-Hill's contract with the Department of Energy included bonuses and penalties based on performance to the contract.

Bonuses on big, expensive projects can be in the range of millions of dollars. In a non-operational state, it cost over $700 million per year to maintain the leaky buildings, monitor and maintain waste containers, and provide security. Kaiser-Hill's bonus for on-time and within budget project completion was $355 million, or about one half of a year's cost to keep Rocky Flats standing.

Additionally, the bonus structure provided that Kaiser-Hill would get to keep 30 cents of every dollar not used in the contract, but would pay a penalty of 30 cents of every extra dollar in total cost overrun. For every day the work extended beyond April 1, 2007, Kaiser-Hill would be docked $54,794. The incentives were substantial for being efficient and finishing under the total contract cost and schedule. Kaiser-Hill passed along the incentives to their workforce by sharing 20% of their profits with employees. The project was completed one year ahead of schedule and $530 million under the contract. The math is easy.

You would think that everyone would be thrilled that the project was completed $30 Billion under budget and 60 years under schedule from the original estimates made by DOE. You would think that the bonus to Kaiser-Hill of $355 million would have been negligible as it was recovered in six months just due not having to maintain the facility. Those involved with the work understood that an incredible event had occurred – it was a crusade based on dedication, and alignment of everyone involved from the Union, management, regulators, the surrounding communities, and state and federal government.

However, the afterword of the project became one of investigations of purported bad contracting with the suggestion that the reason Kaiser-Hill had such incredible performance was because the contract cost and schedule was too high to start with. People outside the project refused to believe that all the factors came together, fueled by the reward of a significant bonus, to create the Extraordinary.

Rather than learning a best practice lesson of what significant rewards can drive, subsequent projects attempted to predict actual cost based on how remediation tasks would be exactly accomplished. This notion of projects with every detail described ignores the human component that creates the Extraordinary. Instead, it treats work as a commodity where the product from low bid will be the same as the result from the highest bidder.

Instead of focusing on the $700 million annual savings from the facility disappearing and the return of a hazardous site to a nature preserve, the naysayers focused on the bonus received by Kaiser-Hill because it was so large. They lost perspective of the cost of non-performance and the motivation provided by a real bonus.

SPREAD TOO THIN

The remarkable success at Rocky Flats has been difficult to duplicate, partially from a lack of focus. At first glance, it seems that this problem would only apply in big organizations; however, it is rampant in our personal lives, work groups, and every size company.

In 1995, the shutdown of the Rocky Flats Plant was a big problem. When the site was first opened in 1952, it seemed to be out in the middle of nowhere. Denver was 15 miles to the southeast and Boulder was about the same distance to the north. However, by 1990, both cities had grown and now were not so far from the site. Hazardous materials continued to be measured in the surrounding land, creeks, and reservoirs. Public sentiment was deservedly negative about what had happened, and the defunct facility created a financial black eye for DOE with a $700 million per year budget just to keep it guarded and contamination contained.

The Department of Energy has a long list of similar sites that are a legacy from how nuclear weapons are made. These sites range from fields to buildings to corners of laboratories. All of these require continual management to protect the current workforce and to prevent spills, leaks, and further contamination due to corrosion and unexpected events such as tornadoes, floods and fires.

For the 10 years from 1995-2005 when Kaiser-Hill was working on the project to reach completion, the Rocky Flats Project absorbed much of DOE's resources. Once it became clear that this project could happen, attention was put on this one trouble spot until it was resolved. As a result, the former Rocky Flats Plant is now a non-issue. 1300 acres of the original site that were heavily industrial remain monitored with a final remediation plan in place, but the remaining 4000 acres were transferred to the U.S. Fish and Wildlife Service as part of a 6,400 acre wildlife refuge.

These days, it is hard to get one big project fully funded because it takes substantial funds from DOE's budget to maintain the legacy sites in a way that more environmental damage doesn't occur. It took $700 million per year to guard and maintain Rocky Flats to protect the public in 1995. Just keeping the materials guarded and the public safe costs $100's of millions of dollars every year with little progress to show toward eliminating the hazard. Big environment remediation projects mean jobs, and every congressional representative wants to keep projects in their state. So, projects happen a little at a time, and more maintenance and preventive projects are worked while waiting their turn for remediation instead of taking on the whole project and gearing up for completion.

However, this strategy is frustrating for workers who feel they are not really making progress. It spends money that could be going for something permanent instead of temporary. It feels like wasted motion with no direction to the real goal. This strategy of spreading the money around keeps everyone marginally satisfied because they are still in business, but in hindsight, projects are not completed and progress is not made toward new projects. Patching up keeps you from gaining on the an end result so that one day, the big problem is resolved and you can devote your funds to new opportunities.

We do this in our personal lives when we hang on to an old computer or appliance and continually waste time and money trying to patch it up. We hang on to relationships that don't really work instead of putting all our efforts into opening up the space for something better. It often seems more efficient to make what we have work than to toss it out and begin again. However, putting away something that has served its usefulness and moving on to what is now in front of us leads to the Extraordinary Life.

LESSONS FROM ROCKY FLATS

I learned two important lessons from the people who were part of the Extraordinary Performance at Rocky Flats. Although I have broken it into multiple plays, I believe they talked about two main themes.

The first theme is that success started and then accelerated when they communicated with people in a way that they could hear. The plays that are about communicating with the people involved are:

- Speaking to the Right Brain with a visual of the end state
- Providing a certain future to shut down anxiety
- Re-aligning each person's perception of who they were in the past workforce to the task at hand
- Providing a forum for people to connect through celebrations
- Creating a game complete with rules and prizes through the bonus structure

The second theme has to do with believing in the power of the positive and having the faith and courage to take action beyond what can be laid out in a carefully organized plan. There has to be some faith in willingness of people to strive for Extraordinary Performance, given the opportunity, a reward, and recognition. It takes a belief that people want to be Extraordinary. The plays about having a fundamental belief that people want to be extraordinary are:

- Listening to their internal wisdom that said the estimates were way off
- Trusting and building relationships with everyone involved
- Believing that a significant reward for the workers would maximize profits for the company and the customer by creating the energy and momentum for Extraordinary Performance

This theme has an age-old dilemma. To get beyond the usual and predictable, you must believe that, given the opportunity, people will do the right thing. You must believe that people want to be part of something remarkable. They want to live Extraordinary Lives. All you have to do is help them.

HARNESSING YOUR HORSEPOWER

INTRODUCTION

Each of us has our personal drive. I like to think of it as our horsepower. Your horsepower is the energy that excites when you meet a new challenge or opportunity. It is the creative spark that fires up your unique abilities to meet the challenge.

You are honing your horsepower with small, everyday challenges as you gain barely noticeable improvement. Then, a problem pops up, and out of nowhere comes an excellent solution, the right people to work with you, and unexpected doors open. All of those little, everyday gains have increased your horsepower.

Harnessing your personal horsepower requires being deliberate. You use your skills to be creative and solve complex problems on-demand – anytime you want. For instance, understanding how to clear your head to make way for new thinking is a skill you need to depend on instead of hoping for the best.

You start to harness the horsepower of other people by describing the future in words that they can hear, whether you are talking about a new world or a new way to cut the grass. You tell a story that inspires them to action.

You have many people that are willing to jump in with help because you have been diligently coaching them to become better. You have systematically shown them who they can be, and helped them grow in skills and as a part of the community, both work and home. You have a supporting team.

You have the credentials and the knowledge to make decisions. Others trust those decisions because you present yourself in a way that creates confidence.

Instead of keeping chores to yourself, you delegate them to those behind you as learning experiences. You pass along the tasks that are no longer a challenge to you so others can build their skills, be excited about challenging work, and build their reputation.

You get out of bed each day knowing that life is about how we embrace challenges and difficulties. You let the world know that you are ready for what it has to toss at you. You look forward to the range of challenges, from mistakes to difficult people to brand-new opportunities.

Your mantra is:
BRING IT ON WORLD! I AM READY TO TACKLE WHAT YOU HAVE TO OFFER TO CREATE A LIFE OF EXTRAORDINARY PERFORMANCE AND EXPERIENCES. BRING IT ON!

PLAY #16

CREATIVITY ON-DEMAND

I have always wanted to draw. I am fascinated by the ability to pick up a pen and create an image that captures the essence of the moment. If the theory of reincarnation is true, I will surely come back as an artist. It's a natural fit because I have already purchased the equivalent of an art store. I have pens, pencils, colored markers, watercolors, and a complete selection of paper. But, alas, purchasing the gear hasn't helped my drawing ability.

I have never been able to draw with any level of skill or grace. Whether it is a lack of practice or persistence, drawing is not my forte. However, my apparent lack of drawing skills has never diminished my yearning to pick up a pen and create an engaging sketch.

Several years ago, I discovered Betty Edwards' book Drawing on the Right Side of the Brain. This classic text teaches drawing based on how our brain works to recreate exactly what we see. Shortly after finding the book, and thanks to an internet search, I was delighted to find that there was a week-long intensive class taught by one of Betty Edward's protégés that promised to jumpstart beginners and take experts to a new level when it came to drawing. It seemed meant-to-be as the class was within the month and a reasonable driving distance from my home. Needless to say, I registered and was soon on my way to Beaufort, South Carolina.

I didn't become any more of an artist because of that week, but one classroom drawing exercise taught me how to access the creative part of Extraordinary Performance. I learned how to become *Creative On-Demand.* The principles I learned in that exercise allowed me to see the usual in an unusual way. I could understand new complex problems and see unique solutions. This play teaches how to turn on creativity and will help you solve difficult problems on-demand in entirely different ways. It is a requirement for Extraordinary Performance. It is the key to seeing the world with new eyes and then being able to lead others along the new path...and do it whenever you want.

The exercise we did was very simple and, in fact, actually seemed to be a waste of time. It took me a while to become engaged, but once I did, it was a life-changing experience. The title of the exercise is Upside-Down Drawing, and it was my introduction to the science of how the brain works. Once I understood the basics of how the brain worked, I learned to write and solve complex problems on-demand. I learned to generate multiple ideas and come up with novel solutions when ever I wanted.

This information comes with a caveat. Science informs us every day of new information about the brain and how it works. The brain is complex and can reconstruct its inner workings to accommodate injuries, aging, and thought processes. There are as many articles discrediting what has helped me as there are articles supporting it. In fact, recent studies reveal that each side of the brain (right side and left side) may have a few specialties, but the original research that suggested significant differences has some faults.

Fifty years ago, brain research suggested that our brains are extremely specialized with the two lobes having specific abilities. Although the physiology of the brain no exactly longer supports that thinking, I believe the tenets taught about human problem-solving and creativity are valuable, and the how-to's of getting to a creative place still work. Although the brain doesn't work quite so either/or as my explanation suggests, I have sound it helpful to humorously label my thinking process. Usually, I am busy executing or I am busy being creative, and the two states don't happen at the same time. The labels Left Brain and Right Brain are my way of paying attention to what it takes to do the kind of work I want to accomplish.

My promise to you is that regardless of the scientific brain research and my simple presentation of how the brain works, the concepts I learned while drawing Upside-Down have improved my performance every day for over 15 years. I know that these concepts will help you too.

BASICS OF CREATIVITY

The reason it is necessary to understand how creativity happens is so you can call up your creative horsepower any time you want. It takes setting up an environment that supports learning new patterns, internalizing new concepts, and putting this information together in new ways. Just as if you were becoming a chef and created your dream kitchen of ingredients, kitchen utensils, and ovens, setting up a learning and creativity environment has a few necessary requirements. If you don't understand the principles, then getting there is hit or miss.

In my discipline of sport psychology, we define learning as a change in behavior. Thus, learning is not reading about a topic or understanding a topic.

We know learning has happened when the performer of a task or behavior does something different.

Education is about teaching new patterns to the learner. Learning means the student can put the new way of acting or thinking into practice. Whether it is formal education where the student receives a grade or on-the-job learning, when a person actually does something differently, then they have learned a new pattern. In the classroom, when students understand the concept to the point that they begin to execute a task differently, they have learned. For example, when a person uses a new way to interact with another person, they have learned a new interpersonal skill.

So how do we learn? Our brain has two lobes or hemispheres. It looks somewhat like a walnut with the shell removed. Since we are discussing the functionality and not physiology of the brain, I am calling the right lobe Right Brain, and the left lobe Left Brain. When it comes to physical activity, we are cross-wired. Cross-wired means that motion of the right side of our body feeds back to the left lobe of the brain. Likewise, the right side of the brain gets the signals from the left side of the body. For instance, moving your right arm is a signal that comes from the left side of the brain. However, everything is not totally cross-wired. For instance, we know now, via advanced medical imaging, vision uses both sides. What you see with your left eye is processed by the right side of your brain with some help from specialty services of the left side of the brain, and likewise for the right eye's performance.

For our discussion, we are most interested in how the brain handles our mental activities. Although the distinctions in the functions of Left Brain and Right Brain are not totally separate, our mental processes seem to operate in two states that have primary functionality on one side or the other.
The key specialty of Left Brain is that for most people, Left Brain is in charge, dominant, and likes to jump into action. Left Brain loves the chirp that lets you know you have a text message. Left Brain leaps at the opportunity to join in a discussion, especially if jumping in means you get away from working on a tedious problem.

Left Brain is the origin of speech and controls the words. Left Brain also likes to pay attention to time and keeps up with time. Left Brain likes life to be step-by-step and in order. It likes to think about what logically should be next.

I think of Right Brain as the center of learning. If we define learning as the embracing of a new pattern so you can recognize it and then use it, Right Brain is where this magic happens. Right Brain is not restricted by thinking about time or about what the next incremental step should be. Instead, Right Brain has no sense of time. Right Brain makes leaps and puts things that seem totally unrelated together. Right Brain is the source of Ah-Ha! moments. The way to talk to Right Brain is through stories, visuals, and solving puzzles.

When it comes to learning, one familiar example is when you are dealing with a new topic. You seem to argue with yourself and work with the pieces until suddenly it comes to you and you understand. But what do you say? You don't say, "Now I understand." Understand is Left Brain language. Right Brain sends the message to Left Brain to say, "Now I see." Right Brain sees, and you have an Ah-Ha! moment.

Left Brain and Right Brain are engaged in a dance. They depend on each other's unique characteristics that combined, lead to Extraordinary Performance. For instance, when solving a tough problem or coming up with a new idea, Left Brain depends on Right Brain to figure out the meaning. Right Brain scours through its patterns to come up with a unique combination that solves the problem. Then when it comes to verbally expressing ideas, Right Brain depends on the verbal capability of Left Brain to express those ideas. Left Brain and Right Brain are a team, but when poorly managed, dominant Left Brain takes over and performance becomes mediocre. Life becomes step-by-step with little innovation.

The fundamental obstacle when it comes to accessing the creative horsepower of Right Brain is that we live in a world where Left Brain is continually called to jump into action. Cell phones, email and text alerts, and open workspaces where you can hear conversations all around create an environment that encourages the dominant Left Brain to stay in charge (which is what Left Brain wants to do anyway).

LEFT BRAIN

DOMINANT

WATCHES TIME

LIKES TO COUNT

GREAT AT MEMORIZED
FACTS AND FORMULAS

CENTER OF SPEECH

RIGHT BRAIN

LEARNS AND SEES NEW
PATTERNS

IS CREATIVE ABOUT
PUTTING THINGS
TOGETHER IN NEW WAYS

ENGAGES IN RICH,
SENSORY PERCEPTION

UNDERSTANDS THROUGH
IMAGES AND STORIES

There are many tasks where Left Brain excels. However, there are other tasks that only Right Brain can accomplish. It takes both sides to create Extraordinary Performance. Luckily for us, the path to managing your brain horsepower is straightforward.

ON-DEMAND HORSEPOWER

It takes two steps to access your horsepower (your brainpower) on-demand. The first step is to convince the dominant Left Brain to shut down so you can fully access the creative and problem-solving abilities of Right Brain. The second step is to deliberately control your environmental calls-to-action that give Left Brain a reason to jump back into control and take over.

STEP 1: SHUT DOWN LEFT BRAIN. Most of our daily activities require that we attend to what is going on around us and make relatively simple decisions. These decisions are ones that we make over and over, and it is simply a matter of deciding. What route should I take home from work? Where should I meet my friends for dinner? Left Brain is in charge for a very good reason. Most of our daily activity benefits from Left Brain's quick action.

The problem is that when we need Right Brain to be in control, Left Brain must be convinced to take a back seat. The concept for shutting Left Brain down to give Right Brain room to work is simple in principle, but can be very difficult to implement. Basically, you simply give Left Brain something to do that is repetitious and boring, and it will shut down. Left Brain likes action, so when you force it to do something very detailed and meticulous, repetitious, or boring, it will drift to the background so that Right Brain can operate at full horsepower.

I often ask my students, "Who does their best work the night before a big assignment or project is due?" From undergraduates to executives, about two-thirds of the class will raise their hand. I then ask them "How would you like to be able to do your best work anytime...on-demand?" All of the hands in the room shoot up.

Here's the secret. For Left Brain to become bored and drift away, it takes about 10 to 15 minutes of doing something repetitious and boring. During the 10 to 15-minute time span, Left Brain comes up with many excuses of other things to do. Maybe you should take out the trash. Maybe you need something to eat. Maybe you should check your email. Wonder what's happening on Facebook? Left Brain is searching for an excuse to jump to action on an everyday activity or decision. So the trick to shut Left Brain down is to ignore all of these calls-to-action and very deliberately just keep working.

One method for shutting down Left Brain when you have new material to learn or implement is to start reading. For each paragraph, by hand on a separate piece of paper, write out the most important concept in that paragraph. Then read the second paragraph and write down the most important concept from that paragraph. I promise that as you begin this process Left Brain starts screaming, "Just pick up the highlighter and highlight the concept. Let's get on with the program so we can get back to doing something more fun!!"

If you continue this process of reading a paragraph and then writing the most important concept by hand on a separate piece of paper, after about five or six paragraphs you'll find that you are just reading, and all of the information makes sense. You are absorbing the information and assembling it into a new pattern. This is when Left Brain has moved out of the way, and Right Brain starts to put together the new pattern. You will be learning at a high level and fast.

When learning math-based technical patterns, the drudgery of working through proofs to create formulas will shut down Left Brain. At this point, Right Brain has the opportunity to see how the formulas work so they can be applied in the appropriate situations. Right Brain always loves a good puzzle.

STEP 2: STAYING WITH RIGHT BRAIN. Let's return to the example of doing your best work at the last minute. Typically, this work being done at the last minute has been put aside because you know it takes a quiet spot and lots of time. Plus, at this late date, you know you cannot get up and leave until the work is done. You are forced to sit there. This is another method for quieting Left Brain. If you are watching the clock or have set a time limit, Left Brain just hangs around waiting for this time of drudgery to be over and done with. To truly engage Right Brain, it is important that you don't have time limits. You will find that without a time limit, you will get the work done both better and faster because Right Brain is working with the patterns and truly learning and creating. So, when you finally close the door and know that you are going to work on your project (or spreadsheet, or performance reviews, or any other activity that requires analysis and thinking beyond everyday decisions), you sit through the 10 to 15 minutes of Left Brain wanting to get up so Right Brain can take over.

Turn off all the distractions that would chirp and buzz to call you back to the world of your friends and putting out fires. Now, Right Brain has a clean, clear, unlimited space to be creative and solve problems.

ON-DEMAND HORSEPOWER WITH GROUPS

When it comes to working in Right Brain space, one misconception is that any speech immediately calls Left Brain back into action. The problem is not the act of talking or listening to speech, the problem is when the speech offers Left Brain an opportunity to engage in something it thinks is more fun than being creative and solving difficult problems.

Many people know the exhilaration of working in a group to brainstorm a new idea or accomplish a big goal. The work accomplished, along with the synergy from working with highly engaged groups, can be a highlight of a career. The key to maintaining this working environment is controlling interruptions and sidebar conversations to stay emotionally connected to others in the group. This flow from working together creates positive relationships and energizes the group members.

Interruptions and sidebar conversations call Left Brain into action. Most of us can recall a time in a group where people were engaged and making good progress. The ideas were flowing and the group was engaged in dialogue, when suddenly someone dropped into the room and said, "Hey, what do you think about the ballgame?" or "Did you hear that John was promoted? Why did they choose John?" or even worse in times of company troubles, "Have you heard anything about layoffs?"

Even if the intruder is asking a simple question about lunch or the company picnic, it quickly destroys Right Brain's problem-solving activity. Left Brain has found an excuse to wake up and take over. It is imperative to silence and quickly usher the interrupter away before the group becomes engaged in talking and thinking about something else and the creative moment is lost.

ON-DEMAND HORSEPOWER FOR STUDYING

I work with many traditional students as well as adult students who have returned to school. I promise my students that I can help them study less, learn more, and perform better in a few easy steps. For those that are willing to follow the guidelines about shutting down Left Brain and clearing out space for Right Brain, the reported results are amazing. I frequently hear, "Why didn't they teach me this in high school?"

I have found some common obstacles to learning. Whether a formal student or not, all of us either need to comprehend new material ourselves or provide that environment for our children, peers, and employees.

STUDYING IN FRONT OF THE TELEVISION/MEDIA. Many of my adult students have children. They often feel they are taking time away from their family and they attempt to study in front of the television or at a nearby table to be in the company of their family. The truth about this type of studying is that the person is not really present with their family sharing the event, nor are they understanding their material. The noise, dialogue, and story line keep Left Brain engaged. I always tease my students by asking them who is a professional highlighter when it comes to reading their classwork. For those that raise their hands, I remind them that the object of studying is not to get the entire book highlighted. When they are in super highlighting mode, it is just Left Brain telling them to mark it up faster so they can hop off to a more fun Left Brain task.

For my adult students (and all students), I encourage them to either be present with their family or to be studying. If they are studying, I encourage them to go to a quiet spot where they can't hear what is going on. Then they must focus on their work without a time limit. Their work will be done better and faster, and then they can actually be engaged with their family during family time.

STUDYING IN YOUR ROOM WHILE YOUR ROOMMATES ARE WATCHING TV OR PLAYING VIDEO GAMES. Left Brain loves television and having people around to talk. On the other hand, Right Brain loves video games where there is a pattern to be figured out. When video gamers lose track of time, their Right Brain has taken over in an attempt to figure out the game's strategy.

If you are in your room attempting to study, but can hear others having a great time, you are wasting your time and effort. Left Brain won't give it up. The call to action is too great.

You are better off to head to the library or another quiet spot where Left Brain can be bored and Right Brain can take over.

If you are trying to get work done in your cubicle while others are talking and stopping by to interrupt you, you are wasting your time to work on Right Brain problems. You'll need to find a space with no calls-to-action and an unlimited time span.

STUDYING WITH A TIME LIMIT. We live in a world of schedules. Schedules are an incredible obstacle to getting in Right Brain space and staying there. My students frequently head to the library to study for two hours (or some other specific time), prior to meeting their friends for other activities. A way to be more effective and efficient with studying is to head to the library and tell your friends that you'll call when done. Leave the ending time open so Left Brain will shut down. Once you have your work done then it's time to go out and play. It is really difficult to convince Left Brain to shut down when there is a time constraint.

MAXIMIZING YOUR HORSEPOWER

Unfortunately, most of us do not have the luxury of setting aside an undetermined amount of time to get to a Right Brain space and stay there. So, here's how to get the right tasks assigned to the right surroundings.

Left Brain activities include editing and checking work, and simply taking care of to-dos that need to be executed. You can do this type of activity in time spans that are constrained (have a beginning and/or ending).

If you have new material to comprehend, writing to do, or analysis to figure out, it requires shutting down Left Brain so that Right Brain is in full control. You'll need to find a quiet spot, hide the clock, and turn off the phone, email, and social media to learn a new pattern or be creative in figuring out new solutions.

We humans are creatures of habit. If you can find a place that you go to regularly to do Right Brain work, your body will make the shift faster. If you have a big project but can't get started, it is because Left Brain is in charge and doesn't know what to do since it is not step-by-step.

TO GET STARTED ON A RIGHT BRAIN TASK:
- Read the documentation and make tedious notes. Left Brain will shut down in about 10 minutes.
- Describe an example or tell a story about the task out loud or write it down. Internal storytelling leaves out too many details and Left Brain just waits you out. For me, I often tell stories or examples to my computer monitor. In just a bit, I am usually typing and my horsepower kicks in.
- If the task is a spreadsheet or analysis, start laying out the forms and be willing to toss the first ones because they are Left Brain's attempts at Right Brain work. Once Right Brain takes over, what you need to do and to accomplish will emerge.

PLAY #17
TELL THE STORY

On a hot day in July 2014, I walked into the AAA customer service center. AAA (American Automobile Association - pronounced Triple-A) is a non-profit member group that provides roadside assistance, maps, and travel guides. Part of the annual membership fee includes free maps and books with extensive, up-to-date information on hotels, restaurants, campgrounds, and attractions for every state. You can drop in to get personalized, detailed trip planning.

I needed AAA. I was days away from leaving on an extended trip from my home in Cosby, Tennessee to Yellowstone National Park with my tow-behind travel trailer. I knew something was up when I couldn't find a parking place. Once inside, I saw the place was packed with people. I asked the lady at the reception desk what was going on to create such a crowd. She replied, "Just a few years ago, it looked like we were going out of business when it came to planning trips. Everybody was using their GPS and didn't seem to need us anymore. But then folks decided that GPS's might be OK for the details of a trip segment, but they still needed a map to understand the whole picture. We are busier than ever handing out maps and helping plan trips."

So, like everyone else, I sat down to wait my turn to get my maps and ideas about the route. When I met the agent, he asked where I was headed. I told him from Cosby to Yellowstone and he pulled out a big paper map of the United States. He took a yellow highlighter and marked my route. Instinctively, my index finger reached for the highlighted line and I traced my way west:

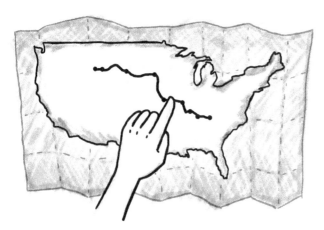

COSBY / NASHVILLE / PADUCAH/ ST LOUIS / KANSAS CITY / SIOUX FALLS / RAPID CITY / CODY / YELLOWSTONE

I was Telling the Story of my trip to my Right Brain.

Most people have a love/hate relationship with their GPS. We love it when we have an idea about where we are going and the kind voice reaffirms what we suspected. It is as if the universal guidance system is providing positive reinforcement about our ability to navigate. That same voice is aggravating, bossy, and persistent when the instructions don't make sense. It is difficult to have faith in a fake voice demanding GO LEFT when our internal compass tells us that we should clearly be GOING RIGHT to get to our destination.

Here's what happened to me at AAA. Our intuitive friend, Right Brain, has no use for step-by-step. Right Brain sees the big picture. Our friend Left Brain likes steps. Right Brain needs to see an image of the entire trip so the steps make sense. The image in this case was a map, and I programmed Right Brain when I took my finger and traced the route. In fact, every day on our actual trip, we took out maps and traced our route to get a sense of what to expect. Not only did we look at the map, we instinctively traced the route with a finger. Without this picture of the trip ahead in mind, Right Brain's internal compass would have continually screeched warnings that we were off course.

For instance, traveling from Tennessee to Yellowstone National Park is a combination of heading West and North. Right Brain is nice and calm as long as the road signs indicate North or West. However, as soon as a road sign is labeled East or South, Right Brain sounds the alarm that there is a problem. Tracing our route each day programmed the nuances of road signs and headings. When we took a southerly path around St. Louis, Right Brain was on board. We had the story in mind.

When you travel purely based on the steps, Left Brain is busy doing step-by-step turns without considering if it makes sense. Right Brain needs the big picture to make sure that each step is feeding into your desired result. Right Brain's job is to insure the steps make sense.

COMMUNICATING WITH THE WHOLE PERSON

To reach the entire person, clear communication takes two completely different forms. The Right Brain's functionality understands an image and the Left Brain's specialty is understanding the steps. The image for Right Brain is an actual picture or a story. The details for Left Brain are detailed steps, schedules, action plans, and budgets.

To really get what you want and where you want to be, you must start with a story for the Right Brain. This story (or picture) aligns the steps with the end result. Without the story of the end result up front, it's anyone's guess as to

what the steps will create or where they will take you.

The work world has a focus on getting things done. Details about a project are action items with their associated cost and a schedule for start and completion dates. The thinking is that if we could just get the details laid out carefully enough, there would be no errors, cost overruns, or slipped schedules. However, all projects seem plagued with difficulties, and when bad things happen, the focus turns to even more rigor in getting the details right.

Real solutions are much simpler when the fundamental problem is understood. When a problem is caused by an incorrect detail, it is not solved by getting even more details. The problem is that the people executing the steps are each working toward a different big picture. Some folks think that lowering cost is the objective. Some folks work toward highest quality. Some people work toward short-term success and some focus on long-term goals. Without the same story of the end result in mind, each person is working the steps just a little differently. They are working to make the steps fit their own story.

BECOMING A STORYTELLER

When I nudge my coachees to become storytellers, they usually say, "How do you come up with a story?" Becoming a storyteller has distinct steps; however, there is a preface to the steps.

PREFACE: Your personal Right Brain needs to have a clear picture of what you look like, sound like, and feel like when you are telling the story. Are you perky and excited? Are you tired or dejected? If you are tired or dejected, no one will really want to hear your story.

Once you have a clear image of you telling your story, you are ready for creating and telling your own stories.

STEP 1: BORING NOT ALLOWED. My family spent a lot of time going to church when I was young. I learned great life lessons and have no regrets. However, our brand of church included long, drawn-out sermons and in those days, there wasn't a kid's service. Adults and kids were all subjected to a dose of boredom several times a week. My first suggestion is a lesson I learned from my hours of seat time spent in church.

NEVER BE BORING.

If you are boring, you are wasting your time and energy, because no matter how important and critical your message is, people don't listen to boring. Can you blame them? I bet you zone out when it gets boring!

STEP 2: BRAIN-TEASERS FOR FINDING THE STORY. I come up with my stories by asking myself three questions. The first two questions help with explaining a point, and the third is for getting everyone on the same path for accomplishing a goal.

One of these questions usually gets me started. It is a method to help me get the point I am trying to make well in mind. I ask myself:

When did what I am explaining happen to me? How did I feel? What was important? What important information did I miss or misinterpret?

What would someone have needed to do to explain this to me? Then I start working on the example, the supporting data, and the benefits of being in the new story.

Wow! I am [in the new world] / [looking at the finished result]! What do I see and how do I describe it to everybody else? Where am I? What is the date? What does the lighting look like? What does it smell like? Who is there with me?

STEP 3: SUMMON UP A DOSE OF PATIENCE. Most of us in live in a world that is focused on getting results as quickly as possible and eliminating anything that is not directly tied, via a step/cost/schedule, to those results. This type of thinking is entirely a result of Left Brain dominance acting out.

The fundamental struggle is to tame the dominant Left Brain so that Right Brain has the space to see the solution. Then there must be enough time and quiet to hear our internal voice tell us the solution. It is as if you must get calm and coax the Right Brain out. The more frantic you are, the harder it is to get to Right Brain's wisdom.

It can be difficult to get everyone to stop long enough to hear your story. You are facing a world where stories and examples seem fluffy because of the perception that anything not fact-based and action-oriented is a waste.

People actually like stories. Once you slow them down and they engage around the story, you will be amazed at how the group pulls together to make the steps all arrive in the same picture. If the end result can be told with an image, it's worth the expense to have a picture of the future created to use a common reference for the group.

STEP 4: GET A DOSE OF COURAGE. *Telling the Story* takes courage. Stories may use some facts to support a point, but the foundation of the story is a description of the surroundings, emotions, motivations, and consequences. Data is safe since it is black and white, and if you are challenged, you can prove your point.

However, descriptions, emotions, motivations, and consequences are never sure. They are interpretations and opinions. You can depend on being challenged when you tell a story. You will need the courage to take the challenges as feedback instead of criticism. You will need the grace to ask for clarification instead becoming defensive. You'll need the curiosity to learn more ideas that support your story and those that disagree with it.

When you *Tell the Story*, it serves as a can-opener to pry open the Right Brains of you and your listeners. You will be amazed at how people will begin to dialogue about possibilities and obstacles once you open the discussion with a story.

I have a tip for learning to *Tell the Story.* One of my own personal coaches told me that my gift was the ability to tell stories to explain my ideas. I honestly believe that this feedback is what took my examples from mediocre to compelling, and a key component of of my best teaching moments.

I spend a lot of time in my car and I listen to storytellers. In particular, since I am from the southern United States with an accent to prove it, I listen to southern comics such as Jeanne Robertson and Jeff Foxworthy. Along with a healthy dose of laughter, I have learned about timing and how to paint a picture with words. I have also learned that a long story is OK if it is engaging.

As you choose who to listen to, always remember that we mimic what we see and hear. If you listen to foul-mouthed storytellers, then the same inappropriate words will slip out when you start telling stories. So, be choosy about what you hear as it will surely be what you say and how you say it.

PLAY #18
THE COACHING CONVERSATION

From our first T-Ball or soccer coach to the person who helps us develop at work or with our families, we love people who help us play better. Good coaches see who we are and who we can be. They push us to be better. It's not always a message of praise, although good coaches sprinkle lots of reinforcement and cheers when we get it right. The secret to being a good coach is seeing and understanding what is happening right now, showing the performer what they can accomplish and how to do it, and then providing feedback on the progress.

Coaching can seem mystical, as if the coach needs to be better than the performer to provide valuable feedback. This thinking is a myth. Coaching is not about relating the coach's personal experience of performance to help another person. Coaching requires understanding the game and the required skills, and delivering feedback on how to become better in ways the other person can internalize.

Coaching has become even more important in the past few years as the composition of the workforce shifts to having more people under age 40 than those over 40 (In July 2015, the composition of the workforce shifted to having more people in Generations Y and Z, the Millennials and younger, than Generation X and the Baby Boomers). For those younger professionals, who are now over half of the workforce, being coached is an expectation. Without guidance from those more experienced who are willing to help them be successful, they will leave for greener pastures. Those in the older half have no expectation of being coached and can even be resistant to coaching others or being coached. Young professionals have been coached their entire life, starting in study sessions with their parents around the kitchen table to make sure they performed well on standardized tests. If they showed an interest or prowess in an activity, they went to specialty camps for coaching in math, music, and many other topics. The under-40 crowd is incredibly coachable. They want to know how they can become better performers, and expect coaching. As a coach, you are helping them harness their horsepower to create Extraordinary Performance.

Coaching is a must-have skill for harnessing the horsepower of individuals to create Extraordinary Performance. Luckily for us, coaching is a planned and scripted activity. The *Coaching Conversations* in this play are designed for on-going personal improvement ranging from correcting problems to discussing opportunities. These Coaching Conversations happen regularly and keep a dialogue going for improving. This play is not designed for immediate corrective or disciplinary action, although you may find the script useful. The three-step process in the play *Delivering the One* negative is used to deliver the message. This play is about categories to discuss in coaching for improvement. Think of Delivering the One as the script for actually discussing an improvement item, and this Coaching Conversation play as the framework for the entire conversation. This play is the framework for coaching and the rules for conducting coaching sessions.

THE COACHING SCRIPT

Coaching is about delivering a message instead of figuring out a format for how to coach people. Most people faced with coaching spend too much time trying to figure out how to do the coaching instead of how to talk about a specific behavior or skill. They don't have a script. Once you learn the coaching script, then your task becomes identifying what the coachee is doing and providing feedback to either reinforce or improve their behaviors.

I primarily teach this script to people who want to coach their younger employees. The script facilitates a structured conversation about work performance. It is personal because it's focused on an individual's performance, but it is not about their personal life. I find that an obstacle to coaching is that people doing the coaching assume it includes conversations about life outside of work and this can feel like prying to the coachee, especially when there is not a base friendship or personal connection outside of work.

The coaching script has three sections. The sections provide for each of the topic areas to discuss with a coachee. Within the topic areas, the Delivering the One play and the methods for delivering valid positive reinforcement with context are used. The three topic areas are:

PACE: Is the person getting enough work done fast enough? How does their output or throughput match up with standards and written expectations?
QUALITY: How does the quality of their work match up to standards?
ORGANIZATIONAL CITIZENSHIP: How is the person doing at being a member of the organizational family?

PACE & QUALITY

Pace and Quality are measurements. These two measurements are a comparison to standards, never to another person. If the work is part of a measured process, then the discussion is about how work actually measures when compared to quotas, schedules, and the process. When work is more abstract, it is tempting to compare the coachee's performance to that of another person. Doing this type of comparison between people can be disastrous to building trust. It sets up a perception of favoritism and suggests that perhaps the coach may be spreading personal opinions among the group. When coaching for performance, comparison must be made to standards. Where there are no standards, the conversation must be around goals that the coach suggests and supports with facts. Comparison to other people almost always backfires as the coachee can readily find reasons that are beyond their control for not performing like another person.

In the case of production-type work where there are set standards for how many items and the measured quality of those items, it is important to spend some time up front teaching the coachee how to find the data that lets them know how they are doing. This education will allow the coachee to become a self-coach by learning how to interpret measured outcomes.

When the work is more abstract without readily comparable outcomes, it is important to teach the coachee to identify what is measureable and then coach for performance to that marker. Schedule and the budget can provide measurable targets. Even though there may not be a consistent measureable item such as parts per shift, more abstract outputs such as creative design and software coding still have deadlines and budgets. It is important to help the coachee understand that they are being evaluated on their ability to do their work within cost and schedule, and when these criteria are unattainable, to work toward changing the expectation. Regardless of the accuracy of the estimated cost and schedule, they need to understand that they will be evaluated based on these targets.

ORGANIZATIONAL CITIZENSHIP

Organizational Citizenship is a fancy way of talking about how people are doing when it comes to being a member of the family. Organizational Citizenship can be used to discuss problems such as poor choices in personal attire and annoying behaviors. It can also be used to encourage coachees to engage in activities beyond simply showing up and doing their jobs.

As the coach, you have the opportunity to let someone know a behavior is annoying to others at work and will eventually impact how they are perceived.

It is a kind way of helping others learn workplace manners. The three-step process for Delivering the One can be used to deliver this feedback.

My favorite example of coaching from the importance of being a member of the family comes from working with a manager who was attempting to have one of his front-line supervisors moved up a step. The supervisor was outstanding at getting work done and working with employees; however, there was a big show-stopper. The supervisor came to work every day dressed with his pants hung low, boxers showing, and shirt tail hanging out. None of this was a safety hazard and it didn't break any written rules. However, any time the manager brought up this supervisor's name for promotion, the other managers wouldn't hear of it. From the supervisor's appearance, the managers didn't believe he was really capable. The young supervisor looked like he belonged on the street instead of helping run a production line. He didn't look like part of the management family.

The manager I was coaching was concerned that any mention of dress would create problems. He didn't want to be negative with such a highly motivated employee, but yet he needed to let the supervisor know that no amount of good work would overcome the perception created by his dress. In a coaching session, the manager and I worked on a script for coaching the supervisor. This Coaching Conversation was designed to let the supervisor know about his excellence in pace and quality, but a problem in being a good citizen of the organization.

When I saw the manager six weeks later, he smiled and gave me a thumbs up. He told me that he had used the coaching conversation we had scripted with great results. He had let the young supervisor know that not changing anything was an option, but that to be a member of the management family, there were some expectations. He told the young man that how he dressed outside of work was his business, but that to be a part of management, he would need to look like a manager. They discussed what this would look like, and a few days later, the supervisor came to work dressed to let everyone know he was a member of management. My coachee laughed and said that the supervisor was teased about being a suck-up and trying to be a boss instead of a regular guy. But, in a few months when the next manager position opened up, the supervisor was promoted. The way the supervisor dressed sent a clear message that he intended to be a part of the management family.

Organizational Citizenship is a great way to talk with coachees about opportunities to grow that are outside of the normal workday. Working on committees to organize functions such as company picnics and 5K's, participating as the United Way representative for their group, and working on behalf of the company in community events sends a signal that a person is there to work toward the success of the organization and wants to be a respected member of the family.

Being a strong performer takes achievement in all three categories to create Extraordinary Performance. Coaching helps people understand where they stand based on their performance on both published and unpublished expectations.

RULES FOR THE COACHING CONVERSATION

A successful coaching program with one or many coachees has three basic rules. These rules for the person who is the coach are designed to make the process efficient and provide value.

RULE 1 – As the coach, you do no preparation for the coaching session. The one thing most of us have the least of is time. If the coaching requires prep work, then the coaching session won't happen, simply because there is not time to prep and do the session. For the first coaching session with someone, take the time to gather any documentation of their Pace and Quality and teach them how to gather and evaluate the data. They become responsible for bringing along performance data to the meeting. Then the coach's job becomes evaluating the data, which can be done in the meeting, and providing feedback.

RULE 2 – At the end of the coaching session, you do not have any action items. Part of coaching is to enable the other person to recognize signals and self-monitor in the future. If you have an action item to help the process, do it in the meeting.

For instance, if you need to make a call of introduction for the coachee, do it in the meeting. At the conclusion of the meeting, you can't have any action items, or coaching will become an unpleasant task.

The purpose of Rules 1 and 2 is to remove the overhead from coaching. Most people have time for a 15-minute conversation. What they don't have time for is an hour's worth of preparation and then 30 minutes of follow-up tasks. As the coachee's manager or perhaps senior fellow employee, you will be able to reflect on the data they bring and what you observe in daily interactions. From everyday life and process reports, you can candidly discuss Pace, Quality, and Organizational Citizenship.

RULE 3 – Sessions are not open-ended. They have a set time of 15 to 30 minutes and a set agenda. Once employees know they regularly have your ear for this time, and the schedule provides time for both a review of their personal performance and discussing for their ideas and thoughts, the drop-ins and hi-jacks of the manager's time stops. Everyone knows when their opportunity is set and will plan to make the most of it.

RULE 4 – Most people like this conversation about their current performance and how they can improve. The research suggests performance is improved when these one-on-one short meetings are held with a regular schedule of one month or less, with a focus on building relationships and improving performance. These coaching sessions are serious business. Starting such a program and then cancelling the meetings signals the relationship killer of contempt, or you don't really matter. The point is not to have long, drawn out meetings about performance. These meetings are a way for people to thoughtfully prepare their questions and ideas, and know that they will have a consistent and frequent time to work with their manager or coach on improving their performance. It is a paradox that adding in these meetings actually frees up a manager's time. However, when employees know there is an outlet for discussion, they refrain from interjecting in large meetings where everyone's time is affected. It minimizes interruptions and turning meetings into problem-solving sessions that really aren't everyone's problem.

   If you decide to do regular coaching, it is a commitment. If you need to cancel sessions, they must be rescheduled as soon as possible.

THE COACHING CONVERSATION PLAY

Just think of it. Your employees are working with you to reach goals. You spend scheduled time each month (or bi-weekly) discussing how to get better. But best of all, you don't dread those conversations because they are not venting sessions. You don't dread figuring out what to talk about because the two of you have something much more important at stake.

DISCUSSION TOPICS FOR THE COACHING SESSION:
- How are they doing at getting the expected amount of work done?
- How is their quality?
- How are they doing at being a key member of the organization?

Isn't this what you'd like to know from your boss? Even more important, you can use this conversation at home. Isn't this what you'd really like to talk about with your family?

FAMILY & FRIENDS COACHING TOPICS:
- How are we doing at accomplishing our goals?
- How is our quality or life?
- How are we each doing at being a good member of our family?

Using this Coaching Conversation format removes hours of trying to catch someone doing something good or bad. It sets an agenda and tone that is about improvement. It is the key lever for working with people as they strive for Extraordinary Performance that leads to the Extraordinary Life.

PLAY #19

WHERE'S YOUR VALUE

People crave feedback. What we really want to know is *Why does it matter that I am here in this group/family? What do I uniquely provide? How else can I contribute?* We want to know what is valuable about us and our unique contribution.

We don't embrace criticism and advice. We want to know how what we do is working so we can better understand what needs work and what is already working. It's not a matter of good and bad. Criticism is a relationship killer and often is based on personal evaluations that end up with giving advice. What people want from feedback is how they measure up to standards and expectations.

Unfortunately, your feedback often comes from people who aren't familiar with the standards and expectations that lead to Extraordinary Performance in your discipline. And when it comes to leadership and making an impact, those providing feedback often mimic the behaviors they learned from watching someone else who didn't know what they were doing. So, most people give feedback without an educated set of skills for helping people improve and make corrections. They evaluate based on their personal experience and knowledge rather than an objective set of standards, and use language that isn't helpful.

For instance, a computer programmer has the unique skill of being able to make software run efficiently. This person's mind can see the wasted steps. They can reduce clumsy computer code to the most basic mathematics rules to create fast running applications. This programmer may work for a career manager – someone who is great at distributing the work, providing resources, and defending their group against political dramas. So, when the programmer asks the manager to provide feedback, their manager has no reference for recognizing the unique technical contribution of the programmer. Their only background for providing feedback is if the programmer meets the schedule and is within budget. A conversation about how to improve never provides valid feedback about the real value of this employee. It is only about the part of their performance their manager understands. To make the feedback problem even worse, managers often comment on discipline skills and talents outside of their understanding, and do it from an uneducated basis. The relationship becomes damaged instead of enhanced.

What appears to be the obvious solution is to only work for managers with expert discipline knowledge. However, this type of manager can be a career-buster. They understand the nuts and bolts of the work, but are not necessarily an expert when it comes to managing their employees or handling the politics of dealing with other managers about business decisions. Thus, their prime employees get little visibility in the organization outside of being discipline experts, and opportunities become limited.

COMPONENTS OF GETTING VALUABLE FEEDBACK:
- **PLANT SEEDS.** First, you must understand how you are unique in what you bring to the organization so you can articulate it to your manager. If your manager knows the key terms, then it's more likely they can recognize opportunities that match your skills.
- **FIND YOUR VALUE.** Ask your manager to provide feedback on how they believe you provide value to your organization.
- **PROVIDE MORE VALUE.** Ask your manager about how you can provide more value to your organization.

These questions and your knowledge of what is unique about you create feedback that reinforces the actions you need to keep doing, and provides information about how you can build on what you already have. It shifts the conversation from being about good and bad skills to a dialogue of where you are and how you can improve. It also provides an opportunity for you to educate your boss about what you really have to offer. When your manager is in meetings and hears key words that describe your skills, your chances of being matched to opportunities increases. Your opportunities depend on educating your manager about who you are, what value you bring to the organization, and how you match up to potential opportunities.

As a young engineer, I immediately began working on my Master's degree in Mechanical Engineering design. My expertise was in performing complex computer analysis of machines. At that time, computers were a tool that only a few engineers could use. Computers were still a specialty of research scientists. I never let my managers know that I was spending my nights and weekends learning these skills and working on major projects as a part of my degree program. Thus, I was never assigned any of this type of work even though it was my specialty. If fact, they hired someone with no knowledge of this sort of work and trained them. It wasn't my manager's fault. It was my problem – I never let anyone know what I was doing and my unique skills.

UNDERSTANDING YOUR VALUE

It can be hard to understand just where you fit with your particular combination of skills and natural preferences. Your skills may lie in solving complex problems or intuitively understanding how to get things done. Your skills may be working with people in a way where they become inspired to join the group to create something new. You may be the master of new ideas or the negotiator who resolves conflicts. You may be competent at almost everything, but there will be a particular area or combination of areas which creates the most value.

If you are fortunate, you'll have a wise mentor who can help you articulate where you shine. Most of us discover our value through reflection and an understanding of the range of talents people have. It also helps to have someone with more exposure to opportunities showing you just what is out there.

A simple process that can help you frame your value is to consider these questions. They provide insights about when you are at your best and when you are not at your best.

SIGNALS THAT YOU ARE AT YOUR BEST:
- When do you have the most energy? The base skills you are using in activities where you are most active in a positive way might be where you bring value.
- What makes the time pass quickly for you?
- What are the scenarios where you seem to get what is happening while those around you are still stumped?

SIGNALS THAT YOU ARE NOT AT YOUR BEST:
- What are the activities that wear you out? At the end of the day, when do you feel unproductive even though you have worked hard.
- What type of dealing with people is unpleasant for you? This feeling can be one of too much or too little because of the number of people, the conflict, or the structure and rules.
- What type of work seems hard and doesn't come naturally? Perhaps these tasks aren't where you'll naturally have insights because the work process doesn't flow naturally.
- What are the scenarios where you really don't care what happens? If what you are doing really doesn't matter to you, then it's hard to be enthusiastic and invested in your work.

We want our significant others, friends, and bosses to let us know what we are best at. It's difficult to rate and rank our own performance. However, determining your best self and your value is your own personal task. Once you figure it out, then it becomes your job to let others know how you can shine and then to manage the responsibilities you assume. The more you are responsible for activities that match your value proposition, the easier life becomes, and the more you shine.

There is one significant caveat to understanding your personal value proposition and insisting on living your life based on that insight. To be incredibly successful, you must be a minimum of competent at every skill. There is no room for poor performance at any skill either in your discipline or in working with or leading others. To make an impact, you are competent at everything you are asked to do, and then there are those things where you bring an additional unique value. You don't have the luxary of avoiding learning and performing activities you don't like simply because they are not your favorites. The goal is competency at everything. There is no room for thinking about strengths and weaknesses as an excuse to be marginal.

ASKING FOR FEEDBACK
ABOUT YOUR VALUE

Asking for Feedback is a two-sided conversation. You have the opportunity to explain some of your unique contributions that provide value as education to your boss. Also, by discussing your value, you avoid a skills evaluation based on the boss' perception of success. The typical request for feedback from the boss goes like this, and you are guaranteed to be frustrated at the conclusion of the conversation:

You get your nerve up to finally walk into the boss's office to figure out where you are lacking. It feels like going to meet the hangman because you have no idea where you are inadequate.

The boss looks up and there you stand...or at the end of a conversation about budgets and schedules, you shift uneasily in your chair and say, "Could you give me some feedback on how I am doing?"

Regardless of how you get to the question, the boss is blindsided. Your manager has been busy thinking about their own personal challenges, and really hasn't noticed anything about you except that you seem to be an OK sort of person and definitely not a problem child. However, since they are the boss, it seems to be imperative to tell you something. So, you get feedback on the last thing they saw or heard that might have been negative:

"Well, I think you take five minutes too long for lunch some days."

Or, "I heard Benjamin mention that your spreadsheet had some errors in it. Maybe you should check your work more carefully."

Your boss has not taken a list of important skills and then observed you over time to understand what you do well and where you can improve. The boss has not spent time with you discussing important milestones and how to get there. Your feedback conversation becomes a review of whatever is most current on the boss' mind, and provides little value. Even worse, you'll feel misunderstood and frustrated from nit-picking. The relationship is potentially damaged.

THE PLAY – GETTING FEEDBACK ABOUT YOUR VALUE

Your objective when it comes to feedback is to understand where you bring value and how you can be even more valuable. Even a discussion of your faults can be about improvement instead of criticism about perceived problems.

STEP 1: SET A TIME IN THE FUTURE FOR A MEETING TO TALK ABOUT YOUR VALUE. Avoid drop-in discussions. Your boss is busy thinking about his or her own dilemmas and problem employees. If you are a good employee that isn't causing problems, your manager is most likely grateful to not be put in a position of being your disciplinarian. Most likely, your boss is not paying attention to how you are good for the organization. Plus, if your manager spends a lot of time dealing with difficult employees, a spur-of-the-moment conversation may end up with confusion due to left over tone and energy. Your potentially positive, career-building conversation may come across as discipline where you get an earful of negativity and no choices, simply because your manager is in taskmaster role from a prior interaction with someone else.

If your boss is an expert in your field, you may receive valuable insights about your expertise, but faulty feedback about your leadership skills. If your boss is an expert manager, you may receive insights about how you fit in the organization, but faulty information about how you actually do your work. Either way, give your boss some time to think about the conversation and set a time to close the door and talk. Spur-of-the-moment feedback is rarely meaningful, and can easily be focused on the wrong things.

STEP 2: PROVIDE YOUR BOSS WITH A LIST OF THE AREAS YOU'D LIKE TO DISCUSS. You will learn much more by providing a list of important topics. An open-ended option of other topics provides a spot for extras, but bounding the conversation will make it much more productive for you.

If you don't have a list of expectations and standards for your particular position, use the categories of Pace, Quality, and Organizational Citizenship which are described in The Coaching Conversation play.

In the area of Leadership, the Ambio360™ surveys provide you with skills and feedback about those skills. Your results from the survey are a great place to ask for specific observations from your manager about your feedback. You can use the free Ambio360 provided at the conclusion of this book as a starting place.

STEP 3: START THE CONVERSATION WITH A DISCUSSION OF THE VALUE YOU BRING TO THE ORGANIZATION. Avoid discussing good and bad or best and worst. If you can talk in terms of what you do well and where you can improve, the conversation can readily move to a discussion of ways the organization can support your improvement. Most importantly, a discussion of your faults and weak skills has an implied sense that perhaps you won't be able to improve. When you talk in terms of what you do well and what you can do better, there is an implied perception that you will be successful.

When you and your boss discuss your value, it opens thinking to other places your skills might be important. A discussion of value creates the positive with implied success.

STEP 4: CONCLUDE THE CONVERSATION WITH A DISCUSSION OF WHAT YOU CAN DO TO BE MORE VALUABLE. This conversation opens doors because it recognizes where you are and also frames where you can be in the future. One reason for having the conversation with your manager or a mentor is to help them frame your potential value.

STEP 5: AVOID THIS CONVERSATION BEING YOUR PERFORMANCE REVIEW. Most professionals have yearly targets for improved performance that are written and discussed as a part of their annual performance review. Performance reviews become legalistic in a hurry as the end result can impact salary increases or even disciplinary action. This conversation about your value is meant to be one that happens regularly so you can internalize how to better help your organization. You are looking for insights and help instead of formal feedback.

It is important to establish a dialogue about where you fit and your unique contributions. Unfortunately, people fall into a trap of thinking that everyone else is like them. These conversations at work, home, and play are a key component to building your Extraordinary Life. When you and your counterparts combine your abilities, skills, and relationships, you start to build something remarkable.

PLAY #20

BEING LEGIT

You must be legitimate. The real deal. *Being Legit* means that your pedigree and credentials support who you say you are. Several years ago, I was at a trade show promoting the Universtity of Tennessee's Aerospace and Defense MBA at an event for companies and people in space applications and space defense. As the program director, I was legitimate because my program's focus aligned with the interest of the crowd, and my proposition of education came from an accredited university. However, I started to understand what it meant to *Be Legit* from a conversation with a young man from the booth across the aisle from me.

A young reservist came over to talk with me about my program. He told me about how he had an Associate's Degree in Business Management from the local community college, and was working on his degree in political science from an on-line school so he could take classes while he was deployed. His goal was to earn his degree by the time he finished his commitment to the reserve so he would be in a prime position to start a professional career.

So far, this conversation made sense. I asked him what he planned to do once he graduated. He told me that he planned to be an engineer. He liked being around the high-tech equipment in his reservist role, and wanted to pursue a career in that field. I suggested that to be an engineer, you need an engineering degree, and he let me know that he was not able to find any on-line engineering degrees, so political science would have to do. He believed that any degree would work because he would have field experience with the equipment. Unfortunately for this young man, he might be able to find a job associated with high-tech equipment, but his education was not going to match up to being in an engineering role, or even a technician role. He was not going to Be Legit. His hard work for his degree was not going to get him to his goal.

Being Legit means that when people see you with your degrees, credentials , and experiences, they immediately understand that you are prepared for that discipline's way of thinking and are engaged in the profession.

THE COMPONENTS OF BEING LEGIT

BEING LEGIT HAS THREE COMPONENTS:
- **DEGREES** – You have the degrees that align with your role/job
- **CREDENTIALS** – You have the credentials that support your role/job
- **EXPERIENCES** – You have the experiences to demonstrate you are engaged in your discipline and on track

Each of these components creates a perception of your credibility to be who you say you are. For instance, I have been fortunate to have lots of opportunities for formal education and experiences. On the next page, you will see an example of my personal introduction and how it establishes credibility. As you follow along, please note how your perception of me changes.

Now, my intention is not tooting my own horn, but to provide an example of how legitimacy is created. Totally by accident, I managed to get organized and pursue activities that contributed to a persona of competence. I remind my family and friends regularly that they should listen to me because I am the one with the PhD. They just laugh at me! However, notice how you started to think about my expertise and credibility as I built my story of degrees, credentials, and experiences. When I use this example in my classes, people become more willing to give my thinking a chance simply because, on the surface, I seem to *Be Legit.*

DEGREES

Maybe what you want to do doesn't require a degree. Maybe you just need any degree, or maybe you need a specific degree to be eligible to enter a professional field. It is important to be frank with yourself about what it takes to reach your goal. In the United States, we love an underdog. We love the millionaire who never finished high school. We believe that anyone can do anything. Unfortunately, this type of thinking leads us to believe that we don't have to follow a set path – we can do things our way and still get to our goal.

Playing the odds is risky when it comes to establishing your professional skills without the necessary degrees. If you work for a large organization, it is certain that they will have policies in place about promotion and job titles that require certain types of degrees. If you are working for small organizations that only care about output, you might get by without a degree or specific

ELAINE'S INTRO	LEGIT CATEGORY	OTHER PARTY'S THINKING
Hello, I am Elaine Seat.		OK, so what. We all have a name.
My BS and MS are in Mechanical Engineering.	Degrees	Wow, she must be smart to have a BS and a MS in engineering.
I am also a licensed engineer in Tennessee and have my PE. (Engineers can take a two-part nationally standardized test based on classroom knowledge and experience. The test is known to be difficult, and passing it lets everyone in the engineering world know that you can do high powered engineering work.)	Credentials	Oh, she is the real deal to have her PE license.
I also have a PhD in Sport Psychology from the University of Tennessee. My associated field is Counseling Psychology.	Degrees	Really, engineering degrees and psychology degrees...so, that's why she can talk about technical people and technical work.
I started as an engineer and then moved to a chief technical engineer before becoming a manager at Lockheed Martin Energy Systems. I had a 20-year engineering career before moving to the University.	Experiences	Lockheed is a high-tech company and clearly she gets being an engineer.
I have been on the faculty at the University of Tennessee for over 15 years.	Experiences	The University of Tennessee is a respected school. She must be talented to be on their faculty.
I started at the University of Tennessee as a National Science Foundation sponsored visiting professor, and then moved to Director of the Aerospace-Defense MBA program.	Credentials Experiences	Visiting professor...a Director of a MBA program...Wow, this lady must be good or she would not have had those jobs!

degrees. However, you start to put constraints around yourself when you are competing with others for positions and, all other comparisons being even, they have a degree and you don't.

There are more and more jobs that require a degree before you can sit for their licensing exams. The degrees that support certifications range from Associate's Degrees to PhDs, depending on the position. If you intend to be a surveyor's assistant or work with concrete pours in construction, being certified to test concrete may require an Associate's Degree plus passing the state exams for that certification. If you plan on being a lawyer, you must have an undergraduate degree to be admitted to law school, and then a degree from law school to take the BAR exam and be able practice law.

It's worth your time to figure out your end goal and learn about the degrees that those positions require. For instance, when graduate engineers want to move to company management roles, they may need an MBA in addition to their engineering degree.

The important task is to analyze where you want to be and then formulate your plan to pursue those degrees.

CREDENTIALS

Credentials are certifications, licenses, and objective evidence that you have the training outside of formal education to support your role and job. Credentials usually have an exam or project where you demonstrate that you understand the material and its application. Another requirement may be a specified length of time as an apprentice or practicing in actual work settings.

Some professional credentials are licenses. There are licenses for Professional Engineer (PE), Registered Nurse (RN), Medical Doctor (MD), Lawyer (BAR), Accountant (CPA), and many more. Although each of these licenses requires extensive education and degrees, passing the license exam lets everyone know that the licensee has met the standards for providing an important service.

Professional certifications typically require passing a standardized exam and often require several years of practicing the profession with letters of recommendation. The PHR certification for Human Resource Professionals is an example of this type of certification, and has a degree in a Human Resource-related field as a base requirement.

There are general-purpose certifications that cross many disciplines. A Program Management certification program (PgMP/PMP) teaches skills in budgeting, scheduling, and managing resources for projects. This certificate applies in all industries and can be a valuable add-on credential for any person that meets the criteria. Another cross-disciplinary certification is a Black Belt. In the workplace, a Black Belt has nothing to do with martial arts. A Black Belt certificate means a person has completed training and evaluation to be well-versed in Lean and Six Sigma methodology for leading improvement projects.

Most of us will need to continue training our whole lives. Certificate programs establish that the training was comprehensive in the topic. The evaluation component insures that the certificate holder actually learned and did the work to become a knowledgeable practitioner.

If your organization provides for annual training that allows you to take a course or two per year, you might consider an organized plan of taking the courses that result in a certification. Certifications can go on resumes and are recognized, while simply attending a workshop or course doesn't provide as much credibility as a certificate.

EXPERIENCES

Your experiences show that you are on track. It's not just any experience, but those that are associated with your dreams and profession. An example that seems unfair happens all the time for single parents. Let's say that a young, single parent of a preschooler is a professional such as an IT specialist, engineer, finance comptroller, purchasing buyer, or supply chain representative. The company has a policy that their future managers spend a year as a front line supervisor on the production line which has rotating shifts and often 12 hour days...with lots of weekends to make up production when there have been maintenance problems.

Our single parent has been asked many times to go and work on the line as a supervisor. However, with a little one at home, the answer is always... *not until my child is older and I am more comfortable with leaving him with someone.* The single parent's supervisor understands and knows that when the time is right, the year on the line will happen. However, everyone else doesn't know the reason, and starts to think *maybe this young person isn't really that good. If they were, then the company would have them doing their time as a front line supervisor.*

The people around us unknowingly begin formulating conclusions based on the experiences a person is provided. Sometimes we pursue these experiences ourselves, and sometimes our organizations offer them. But either way, people are subconsciously noticing who is doing what and their automatic tracking system whispers where the careers of those around them are headed.

BEING LEGIT   181

You can help create experiences by proposing activities and job assignments that suggest what you are actively pursuing. For instance, a production worker might ask their manager if they can participate on a team that is deciding which equipment to purchase or how to better schedule work. A front line supervisor can ask their manager for the opportunity to fill in when they are absent. Professionals can request attendance at conferences and trade shows to expand their knowledge of what is new and upcoming in their field. Young professionals can request to tag along with more experienced employees on visits to other sites.

However you take action, it is important to understand what kind of experiences let everyone else know that you came to play and are excited about harnessing your personal horsepower to achieve Extraordinary Performance.

PLAY #21

PASS ALONG THE BORING

Delegation is often touted as providing two helpful benefits for a manager. First, delegation is pitched as a good way to prepare others so they can gain experience and prepare them for upcoming assignments or roles. It can be a strategy for helping people develop their expertise and exposure. A second benefit of delegating tasks is to free up time and horsepower for you to take on new challenges.

Feedback scores from the Ambio360™ survey reinforce the notion that it is difficult to pass along a task. The Ambio360 survey is provided as a part of this book as a tool to help you understand your leadership skillset. Information on using the survey is in the last chapter. From the manager/professional survey, a top-10 Needs Work item is *Micro-manages when really interested or stressed about a task,* and the #3 Needs Work behavior from the general purpose survey is *Gets bogged down in details.* It's hard to pass along something we know to someone else. It's even harder to pass it on to someone who isn't an expert at the task. It is difficult to take the risk of a poor quality outcome because the person the task was delegated to doesn't know the idiosyncrasies or might not work fast enough to complete it on time. Frankly, it's difficult to summon the patience to explain and coach someone else to learn the task when you can do it yourself in less time than it takes to teach them. Plus, doing it yourself, you'll know it has been done correctly.

Whether you are a manager trying to free up time or a professional with too much to do, delegation provides help for getting tasks done. This concept sounds great. Who doesn't want to get everything done and have time for new challenges? The problem comes in knowing what to pass along and in being comfortable with the learning curve as novices struggle with a task that is a no-brainer for you.

Both managers and professionals seem to continually accumulate tasks. Particularly in the first levels of people and project management, managers are plucked out of the ranks of workers because they are good at getting things done. There are usually a few tasks that no one can imagine anyone else doing, and these tasks stay glued to the rising manager. So, along with a new position, star performers tend to keep some tasks that eventually become ankle weights by taking away time, focus, and energy. These artifacts from a prior position distract them from their new role.

The problem is not always thinking that other people can't do the task. The problem is twofold. First, the expert knows they will get the task done correctly and in a timely fashion. They have done it lots of times. They know the background, the pitfalls, and what's meaningful. They know there will not be mistakes, the painful calls about rework, and potential strife with the person receiving the output. At first it can be very difficult to pass along a task to someone that's not familiar with it simply because of the potential hassle that might be involved with getting it done correctly and in a timely manner.

Secondly, the reason it is difficult to pass along the task is that most tasks that are ready to be passed along have become incredibly boring to whoever is doing it. It can be difficult to hand-off a task that you actually dread doing yourself. Many kind-hearted bosses keep these tasks because they do not want to impose on their employees, and then, combined with the first reason, their logic becomes, "This is really unpleasant to do and I can get it done quickly. I don't want to saddle one of my employees with this task because it's not any fun."

This self-talk is faulty thinking. Here's the better way to think about passing along a boring task. I'd like for you to recall a time when you were given a task you did not know how to do. Perhaps you spent long days or maybe even a weekend figuring out how to do this complicated task. It was a challenge, but by the time it was finished, you were proud of your efforts to get the task done. Your confidence was boosted because you had learned to do something new. It seemed to demonstrate your value to your organization that you could take on more complicated work.

When you think back on those tasks, you'll recall that there was someone more experienced than you who could have done that task easily. They would not have made the novice mistakes. They would not have needed to ask so many questions, and they could have done it within regular working hours. In hindsight, you'll probably recognize that the actual task you did was not special. It was your willingness to work on it and figure it out that mattered. Your willingness to make a personal investment that went beyond the usual effort demonstrated that you were up to more challenges. Most of us recall these tasks that were challenges to us as some of the best times in our career.

So here's what I believe happens. When we have a task that is boring, we forget that at one point it was a challenge to us. We forget how proud we were to first demonstrate accomplishment and, eventually, mastery of that task. The evolution of learning a task is such that when we start it, there is a tremendous challenge. Our job satisfaction skyrockets because we are required to demonstrate just what we can do and have the opportunity to prove our value. Once we have done the task many times and learned the rules, the exceptions, and the process, it becomes routine. We have achieved mastery. In the course of a day, it is actually rewarding to have a task that keeps us on our toes but doesn't have the stress of the unknown. It is a task that we don't dread. It's just one that we do well and we are reminded that we are indeed a valuable part of the operation.

The days roll along, we do our routine tasks, and crank out the work. And then one day that task that started as an exciting challenge and eventually moved on to satisfying mastery, becomes pure drudgery. We dread the task showing up in our queue because it's taking us away from something new that challenges us. A new task provides excitement from the challenge of learning. Although we realize it's important, we begrudge that the old task takes up part of our day and part of our horsepower.

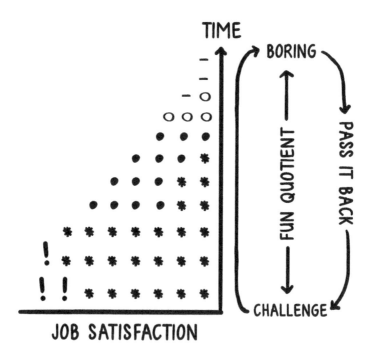

A delegation strategy that works to get work accomplished and also builds relationships is what I call *Pass Along the Boring*. Whether you are a manager or a professional, notice when a task has become boring. Notice when you begrudge the time and energy a task takes, but you're doing it anyway to get it done and done correctly. If you are continuing to do the task because you don't want to impose on someone else by asking them to learn such a boring task, you have a loud and clear signal that it is time for this task, which is boring to you, to be passed along to someone that will find it a challenge.

We become engaged with work and excited about what it has to offer when part of our day is a challenge. When work becomes simply executing a series of tasks that we already know how to do, it becomes drudgery and we feel like robots. Even when the task requires thinking and judgment, once we know the ins and outs of decision-making for the task, it becomes boring and work becomes a chore.

So, engage your workforce by identifying tasks that are drudgery or boring to you, and then pass them along. These are most likely tasks that you have done long enough. Your skill set has reached full benefit of doing the task as you've gone from the stage where the task was challenging through the mastery stage, and then arrived at the boring stage. To identify the right person for handing off this task, recall your experience level when the task was new to you and was a challenge. Recall yourself at the time you learned the task and find your clone. Arrange for that person to take on your task. You lose the boring and they get a boost.

Once you pass the task along, be willing to let them work long hours. Although some people recommend that you let them make the mistakes for themselves, I have always appreciated what my first boss did for me. There is a fine line between meddling and mentoring. Making sure a person's reputation is not damaged by a first time performance on a task is a great opportunity for coaching.

MENTORING AND DELEGATING

As a young engineer, my first job was to write technical specifications for purchasing machine tools. If you are not in manufacturing, you might not know what a machine tool is. Machine tools are the machines that make parts that are assembled into final products. Machine tools physically create the products we buy. Tremendous design goes into the mechanical parts of machine tools, their electrical systems, and their controllers. Machine tools are incredibly accurate in what they make. In fact, these complex machines must be over 80% more accurate than actual parts they make so that when all the parts come together, the final assembly is sound.

My first role as an engineer was working with our machine shops to understand the parts they were planning to make. Then I would determine the kinds of machine tools we needed to cut the curves, drill the holes, and create our parts.

The output of this task was written documents, sometimes in excess of 50 single-spaced pages, that described these machines in a very detailed manner. I designed the mechanical part of the specification and would work with our electrical and controller engineers to develop specifications for their parts of the machines. The machine tools being purchased by these specifications ranged in price from $20K to over $5 million. Getting the machine right was a big deal because they were very expensive and crucial to our mission. There were no second chances if we made a mistake and designed the wrong thing.

Once the document describing the machine tool was completed, I sent it to everyone that had a role in procurement, installation, maintenance, and use of the machine. The document would go to over 25 people for scrutiny, and then through a second approval cycle once all comments were resolved to everyone's satisfaction.

I resented a requirement from my supervisor. My supervisor told me as soon as I started working that I could not send out any documents and any technical specifications until he first reviewed it. I was insulted by this requirement. I was not very happy that somebody was reviewing my work. He had done my job previously and worked with machine tools his entire career, but appeared to me to be nit-picking with the comments he made. He was picky about my writing, the way I described the machines, and the way I described the accuracy and final testing specifications.

Although he was always kind and provided his feedback with details about why he made his comments, I felt that I was under continual scrutiny. However, after a couple of years, he let me know that I had learned my job and was producing high-quality work. My specifications were top-notch, and mistakes he found were not errors of judgment or errors of inexperience, but were were simply mistakes anyone might make in such a complicated document. He also let me know the reason that he had insisted on reading my work carefully and making corrections before the document ever went to the eyes of 25 commenters. The year was 1980, and he knew that some people didn't think women were capable of being good engineers. He wanted the other professionals working with me to believe that I was competent. He didn't want anyone to see my rookie mistakes and have an excuse to doubt my ability. He did me a tremendous favor by making sure that I was perceived to be the real deal as a woman engineer from the work I performed.

My supervisor didn't do my work for me, but he reviewed it and worked with me to understand the discipline and to produce quality designs. He became my friend, and I have always respected him for making sure I got off on the right foot.

When you pass along work, especially to younger, more inexperienced people, the trick is that you do not tell them how to do the work. You send them off with an example and tell them where they might find other information. Then, you take your years of doing that work to ask very good questions to help guide them in how they make decisions.

All of your expertise becomes your inside information. You use it to help bring them along in a way that brings them confidence, and demonstrates to everyone else that they are the real deal. Not only will you create more time for yourself by passing along the boring, you free yourself for your next challenge.

It's a cycle. When a task becomes boring, pass it along to someone that is up for the challenge. Then ask your boss for your next challenge. With the challenge comes job satisfaction and the knowledge that you are part of the lifeblood of your organization.

PLAY #22
BRING IT ON!

One of my favorite coachees was scheduled to call at 9 am. He was an energetic man who thoroughly understood his business. He could run the equipment and keep his team on task to meet their targets. I was surprised when 9:30 came and went and he still had not called. Finally, about 9:45, the phone rang and it was Tyler. He quickly apologized for missing our scheduled time, and explained that the cause was an unexpected problem on the shop floor. It took several minutes for me to convince him that it was OK to be late because I understood that his work was important. But Tyler was frustrated that he seemed to be hi-jacked every day by something that was unexpected. He felt that he had let me down by being late, but would have let his team down by leaving for our phone call. He seemed on the verge of tears because he couldn't keep everything running smoothly.

Being late for our session wasn't the first time Tyler had been stressed during a coaching session. When we met in person, I insisted that he turn his phone off so we could focus. Once the phone was off, he calmed down and we developed a great plan for improving how he coached his workers to be able to run the process on their own. I learned from my coaching experiences with Tyler that sometimes it is not the actual problems that are trouble, it is a person's perspective on problems.

Tyler had internalized that his goal was to have all problems solved so that each day he would show up, make a few decisions about how to handle work for folks who called in with absences, and then watch his process run like a fine-tuned machine. He had conducted Lean events to remove waste, had statistical charts showing exactly where he was on productivity, and had hand-picked his front-line supervisors. He was as stressed as anyone I've seen as his phone just kept ringing due to reported problems and the plant management breathing down his neck. He was annoyed at the causes of problems and embarrassed by upper management knowing that things on his line were not perfect.

I don't think Tyler was a perfectionist. I don't think his problem was his tendency to micro-manage. Tyler's problem was based on his belief that if he just worked hard enough and smart enough, there would be no problems. Thus, the relentless onslaught of things gone wrong was taking a toll. He believed that processes and people could be organized into a smooth-running machine, and he was wearing himself out with his attempts to get the next problem solved as if it would be the last. He was damaging relationships by lashing out at those who had the problem, reported problems, or inquired about why there were problems.

To make matters worse, Tyler had this same problem at home. He had no patience with his teenage children as they made the usual mistakes of growing into adulthood. He had become an ogre in the house from his disgust at how things couldn't get to smooth sailing.

Tyler needed a new perspective on the nature of life. Rather than be angry at the onslaught of problems, he needed to smile and say, "Bring it on."

Thinking that problems can be eliminated and our everyday lives will run smoothly is not a new perspective. We purchase gadgets and change our routines continuously to make life easier. In the workplace, we have new machines performing the routine tasks, and computers recording information non-stop. All this information leads us to believe that if we can just find the root cause in those numbers, we can fix the problems. We are told the data is explaining what is happening and, with analysis, we will be able to predict the future based on past events. We want to believe that smooth sailing is just one analysis away...or maybe two or three. We are totally unprepared for a continuous stream of problems.

We have two dilemmas when it comes to dealing with problems. First, there are two types of problems, and most of us are focused on how to solve one type. When we try to solve every problem using our one method, we end up with some solutions that don't really work. Second, we have an expectation that we can get all the problems fixed and then life will be smooth sailing. Thus, we are frustrated when problems keep popping up.

THE PROBLEM WITH PROBLEMS

The problem with problems is that it takes different ways of thinking to solve different types of problems. Most of us have been trained in analytic problem-solving methods that are intended to take an existing system and tweak it to eliminate waste; get around a barrier; or plan on how to use our existing resources to solve an upcoming change. The analytic method is based on gathering all the facts, sorting through them to keep what seems valid while discarding the rest, and then working the remaining information like a jigsaw puzzle to come to a better solution for the next time. There are lots of methods for analytic thinking, and it is the basis for almost every problem we have to solve and every decision we have to make. Analytic thinking focuses on improving a process.

Then there are those problems that need totally new perspectives. Just tweaking the old ideas isn't enough anymore. These problems need an intuitive way of thinking that is totally opposite to the analytic method. The analytic method seems risk-free and sure since it is based on facts. And, the solution about what to do in the future feels sure because it is also based on facts. On the other hand, the intuitive method takes logical leaps where the facts don't build to create the next step. It is about exploring completely new solutions while the analytic method is focused on optimizing current solutions. The intuitive system feels uncertain and risky because there isn't a factual foundation.

Solutions created by the intuitive method create new ideas. Solutions created by the analytic method help new ideas become better, faster. You may think this problem-solving discussion isn't really something you use; however, we solve problems every day. Analytic problem-solving looks like this:

There is road construction today on my usual way home. I think I'll take another way that is a little longer, but should keep me out of a long traffic jam (simple analytic thinking).

We need to get these reports done by noon and don't quite know how long it will take. Let's start on them first this morning to get them out of the way, and then move on to our other work (simple analytic thinking).

We are spending money on printing our manuals, and with the new tablets we could quit printing them. Instead, we can upload our documents and then our trainees can use the tablet to take notes on the online presentation slides, and then email the file to themselves. We can pay for the electronic tablets in six months with printing costs and labor to handle it. It will be a cost savings plus the class participants still have the same thing. It's the next step in using technology (analytic thinking about process improvements and eliminating perceived waste).

Intuitive problem-solving focuses on the person using the system and what they need for effective interaction with the process. It starts without a preconceived perspective that the current process simply needs tweaking or the next iteration. While most problems require analytic thinking, there are always problems that need intuitive solutions. Unfortunately, it is difficult to see these types of problems that need this completely different way of solving problems – intuitive thinking. Intuitive thinking doesn't work as an alternative for analytic thinking. It is used for a different type of problem, the ones that just aren't working because people can't or won't use the current system.

EXAMPLES OF WHEN INTUITIVE THINKING IS REQUIRED ARE:
- Developing new products
- Developing new processes to support projects that are different than what is currently being processed
- Designing processes based on how people interact with the project's throughput

I started my career as a design engineer, and without knowing the difference in types of problem solving, I saw every problem as one that needed a brand new idea and used intuitive thinking, when often, all that was needed was simple, analytic solution to get rid of a sticking point. Lots of times I made a mountain out of a molehill when just a simple tweak was all that was necessary. On a few occasions, I was able to see a totally different way of doing business because intuitive thinking was needed. I have always believed that my early experiences as an engineer gave me a human-centered perspective, which resulted in re-designs around the function instead of another iteration of the current process.

As a young engineer, I was given the task of designing a glovebox where parts would be unloaded, measured, and then put in a protective container for storage. I knew that floor space was limited, so I put my thinking hat on and solved this problem like a puzzle where, depending on the part of the process you were working on, you would use different combinations of gloves and positions. I was totally focused on designing to the smallest footprint yet providing comfortable access for the operators, instead of simply making another version of the same gloveboxes we always designed in just another length.

Glovebox design is tricky because technicians can't get much work done if their arm must be outstretched to reach their target. Strength and leverage in your hands goes down as your arms stretch out, so activities need to be done within about 20 inches of the outside walls to have any gripping or lifting power. Thus, if it is a two-handed task, the work-pieces must be even closer to the outside walls. Additionally, attempting to do anything with the thick rubber gloves used in our process made it even more necessary to use two hands or a tool that helped with positions and leverage.

I designed my glovebox with four ports and plotted out the order of events to accomplish the task. I added in features to help with positioning, reaching, and having the leverage to use tools. It was a nice design. The shop management approved my design, but since it looked like a traditional glovebox, they really didn't think about all the changes I was proposing about how they did work.

In the months required to purchase, construct and install gloveboxes, my new process was forgotten. However, soon after it was installed I was called to come down to the shop to explain what I had done. The manager and operators were not very happy.

What have you done! The gloves are wrong handed, and we can't reach the latches. Plus, we can't see our gauges to inspect the parts. What were you thinking?!

I was taken aback by this problem and quite concerned that I had wasted lots of time and money. Plus there wasn't time for a new design because of the production schedule. I asked the machinist to show me the problem. He walked up to the glovebox and stuck both arms in the two ports closest to the end and waved his arms around to show me that he couldn't do his job. Then he walked down to the end of the glovebox closest to the front and showed me the same problems.

I'll never forget my relief. Whether the end user really didn't notice my new design during the review phase or time had caused them to forget, my new way of thinking wasn't being used. It looked like a disaster. However, I let the operators know that the ports were not to be used as two simple pairs, but instead provided single arm access for some tasks and two arm access for others. Once I talked the operator through my scheme for how to use the glovebox, it was a hit. The process had not been obvious without an explanation.

The problem with problems is not the 95% of them that come along and a little analytic thinking comes up with a solution and it's back to work; it's the 5% that need intuitive thinking and are hidden amongst the majority. These 5% create headaches when the analytic thinking is applied. The solution generally becomes messier and messier as patches are implemented in an attempt to solve the parts that just aren't right.

A first step to telling the world to *Bring It On* is to recognize those problems that simply need to be worked out or those problems that need an entirely new idea. A simple way to decide if a problem is in the 95% is to ask the question, *Is this problem part of making the process a well-oiled machine?* If so, it needs analytic thinking. If the answer is I'm not sure why we are doing this, then there is a good chance that intuitive thinking will be needed to solve this problem.

BRING IT ON

I learned an important lesson from one of my students who came to class visibly shaken. The week before, a tornado had blown most of his home away. The floor and walls had been poured 40 years ago from concrete, and all that was left standing were the walls with empty holes for the windows. A house built like a fortress had only the outside shell left, while their outbuilding about 100 feet away was unscathed.

This event happened a few months before my coaching call with Tyler. Mother Nature provided an insight to a perspective on life that changed how I coached him. I reminded Tyler that it was impossible to get everything in its place where there would be no more problems. It is the nature of life that we disagree, some person or part is too stressed and breaks, and something new comes along that changes everything and the analytic thinking kicks in to start making the new run smoothly once the errors appear.

Problems are the nature of life and it is our choice how to think about them. My student lived in a fortress of a house. His family had a good roof, strong walls and a solid foundation, but none of that mattered in a tornado. Whether it is building a home or managing your work, you can never reach a place where there are no problems. It is how life is. The point is to decide how you will embrace problems because they are sure to come.

I encouraged Tyler, and I encourage everyone I coach, to get out of bed every day and tell life to come on and bring the biggest, ugliest problem because you are going to solve it. I reminded Tyler that he was put in his position because of his expertise at solving problems. He had a better job than most people and had been placed in a position that was a trouble spot because of his expertise. He was being paid to solve big problems.

We build relationships around reaching solutions together. Problems are meant to be embraced rather than dreaded and the source of frustration.

I want to clarify that I am not encouraging you to seek out trouble or take risks that cause damage. My point is that problems are sure to come. If you embrace the ones that come your way instead of being angry about them, you'll be clear-headed and better able to find solutions. It only wastes time and destroys relationships to be bitter and angry about a surety of daily life and work.

THE PLAY

STEP 1: Get out of bed every morning with a curiosity about what problems life is going to throw at you today. Be excited to face the challenges ahead because growth comes from challenges.

STEP 2: When you are confronted with a problem, smile to let the world know you can tackle it and reach a successful conclusion.

STEP 3: Decide if you need analytic or intuitive thinking to solve this problem. Ask the question: Do I need a new idea here or do we need to fix this idea so it works better?
- Analytic thinking is needed to fix or optimize an existing idea. Ask questions about the facts and current status to determine waste, changes, and incremental steps to create a finely-tuned process.
- Intuitive thinking is used to come up with new ideas. Ask questions about how the end user interfaces with the problem, and be willing to listen to constraints and start with a clean sheet. It's nearly impossible to come up with new ideas if you are looking at a previous solution. Previous solutions drive incremental changes.

STEP 4: Ask questions that shut down Left Brain's incremental thinking and open up Right Brain.
- Ask How. How can we do this? Asking How implies that you will be able to reach a solution or goal.
- Don't ask for the reasons not to. Asking people to provide the reasons something won't work at the beginning of problem-solving shuts down Right Brain and leads us back to what has been done in the past. Many technical people jump to discussing what will go wrong and why solutions won't work instead of discussing how to make them work and generating options.

AFTERWORD:
PLAYING THE GAME

Hopefully, as you have read the plays in this book, you have realized that the quality of your life and your relationships is totally up to you. You can decide how to interact with others to create joy, impact, and Extraordinary Performance. You choose how to think about what happens to understand the opportunities and how to cope with the challenges.

My undergraduates say it best as they reflect over a semester-long version of the plays and thinking in this book. Their closing assignment is to grade their personal change and to identify the two most useful things they have learned.

Regardless of the grade they give themselves, almost without exception they are amazed how much they have changed. They get it that knowing what they do well and what they need to work on from the Ambio360™ started their specific change process. They understand that although they don't have their new skills mastered, they wouldn't have gotten started and changed anything without the class. Many of them talk about how stopping their nasty habit of giving advice has improved their relationships with their friends, and learning to reflect emotion has repaired tenuous ties with their parents and opened up a fun dialogue.

Since it is a class assignment, they are required to take the Ambio360, do the worksheets, and practice the plays. We role play to practice the methods and set aside embarrassment at not knowing what to do. It is a safe learning environment with lots of laughter and learning from the mistakes. Holding the gradebook is a powerful tool when it comes to encouraging people to learn new skills, and I make it worth their while to try out the plays. I'm also there to coach them in person through the rough spots and to dialogue about what might work better.

I can't force the readers of this book to try any of these plays. I can't force you to move beyond an academic exercise. But, I have a horde of university juniors and adult executives that would tell you in a minute that these plays changed their lives. Being positive instead of critical helped their teams not only perform, but actually enjoy working together. Learning communication skills changed their relationships with significant others, parents, and children. These plays will work for you too.

I have been learning and refining the plays for over 20 years. I am a different person now, and the change was deliberate. So, if you feel stuck, try a play. It changes the dynamic because when you change, those around you are forced to act differently. If you are on your way, I hope these plays provide some additional insights and move you along quicker.

There are lots of perspectives, ideas, and thoughts on how to create Extraordinary Performance, but these are the ones that helped me the most as I became determined to not stay stuck where I was. These plays will get you started and lay a foundation for your Extraordinary Life.

THE AMBIO360™

USING THE AMBIO360™ TO GUIDE CHANGE

The Ambio360 is an online survey that provides you with information about how other people view your skills for working with others and tapping into your creativity. Most people don't have a clear view of how they are seen by others. What we see when we look in the mirror is not how others see us. Gaining an honest view of yourself is a key ingredient for growing as a person.

This survey is used by large companies as tool to help people understand their performance. During the last 10 years, over 5000 people have used the Ambio360. A version of the survey is included with this book so you can learn information about yourself. The survey is simple to use and most people learn that they do lots of things really well and have a few places where they have opportunity to improve. I had my first experience with the value of this type of survey as a leadership coach for MBA students.

In my role as a faculty member at the University of Tennessee, I provide individual coaching on leadership and life skills for MBA students. MBA students are earning their Master's Degree in Business Administration. Many MBA students have a business undergraduate degree and are developing more skills However, an MBA degree often provides students from fields such as engineering and liberal arts with the knowledge it takes to successfully lead and manage a business. At the University of Tennessee, we have a range of MBA programs from the traditional college experience of full-time school to programs for working adults where they come to campus several times during a year, and many classes are provided online. Traditional MBA students are typically younger and have either recently completed their undergraduate degree or have worked for a few years and decided to come back as a full-time student to earn an MBA degree. These students are at the beginning of their professional careers and usually have had little exposure to developmental training and feedback. Most of them have room to improve on just about any leadership and management skill.

I served as a coach these young traditional MBA students several years ago. At the beginning of the school year, the program director would tell the students that faculty who were professional coaches would be delighted to work with them at no cost during their MBA program. All they had to do was to sign up. Typically, three or four students would sign up to work with me as their professional coach.

The student would set an appointment and come to my office. I would start the conversation with the simple question, "How did you come to be in this program?" The student would tell me some of their life history, their educational background and why they were pursuing an MBA degree. My next question would be, "Tell me, what would you like to work on?"

The typical response was, "I don't know. I must be doing pretty well to have been admitted to this program." They would think for a few minutes and finally say, "Everybody needs better presentation skills. I guess I'd like to work on improving my presentation skills."

I also coach in our Executive MBA programs where the students are an average age of 40 and many of them hold executive positions in their companies and organizations. These executive students often have hundreds of hours of training in management and leadership development, and are well versed in their roles when it comes to managing and leading people.

One of the significant differences in our traditional MBA program and executive MBA program is that on the first day, the executives complete several assessments that help with understanding who they are, and they also initiate a 360-survey. A 360-survey (also called a multi-rater assessment) is an assessment where the user rates their own skills in leadership and management and then asks people who know them well to also fill out the same assessment about the user. When the results come in, the user can compare how they see themselves to how others perceive them.

Most assessments, such as StrengthsFinder and the Myers Briggs Type Indicator®, are self-reporting. That is, the person simply assesses how they perceive themselves to be. However, a 360-survey adds an important dimension to self-awareness. It lets the person at the center of the survey understand how others perceive them. They now have the inside information on themselves. They now know what everybody else already knows about them.

When my executive MBA students arrived at my office for their first visit, the conversation went like this: "How did you come to be in this program?" The student would tell me some of their life history, their work history, their educational background, and why they had decided to return to school for an MBA degree.

My next inquiry would be, "Tell me what you would like to work on."

At that point, the student would whip open their notebook containing all the assessment results. They would go directly to their 360-survey, point at a category where their results showed room for improvement, and say, "We have to work on this skill. If I don't get this fixed it will hold me back."

My introductory coaching questions are always the same. *How did you get here?* and *What would you like to work on?* My first question always seemed to elicit about the same story from both the traditional and executive MBA students. But I began to notice a pattern of difference in responding to my second question. Why did my young coachees not have ideas about where to start improving, but my more experienced coachees jumped right in with specifics that needed improvement? Then, after coaching many people, it hit me one day. It wasn't experience that let my executive coachees know what to work on and also created so much motivation for improvement. It was the simple fact that now they knew how others perceived them. From the 360-survey feedback, they now understood what they did well and what they needed to improve. The younger, traditional MBA students had no feedback to create insights about where they needed improvement.

At that point, I vowed to myself that everyone deserved to know how they were perceived by others, and I would help them find out. Everyone deserves to know what they do well and where they have opportunities for improvement. Once a person has the inside information on their skills, they know what to focus on for improvement.

LESSONS FROM THE AMBIO360™ SURVEY

In 2005, I created a 360-survey called the Ambio360. The sole purpose of the Ambio360 is to let people in on what everybody else already knows about them. It provides feedback at a very specific skill level so deliberate action can be taken to improve. I believe that real change is accelerated and easier when people understand exactly what to work on. This project was not my first experience with developing 360-surveys.

In 2000, I worked with a team from Columbia University and the University of Pittsburgh on a grant from the National Science Foundation. The purpose of the grant was to develop a 360-survey for engineering students that would serve to alert them to professional workplace skills. These smart, young people tended to be so focused on problem solving that they became incredibly self-focused and competitive. Engineering classes provided feedback on their problem solving abilities via their grade, but students did not receive any feedback about their ability to work with others. We knew there was more to the story, and our intention was to use the survey to help engineering students working in teams to understand the implications of their behavior and pinpoint strengths and weaknesses.

My part of the project was developing the list of people skills the students would need when they entered the workforce. My team of Industrial/ Organizational Psychology PhD students referenced Department of Labor technical job descriptions for engineers to create a list of specific skills for working with people and self-management. However, when we looked at the final list of skills, it was obvious that it wasn't just engineers that needed all of these skills – it was everybody. From my experience with this grant, I learned there was a common set of skills everyone needed for people interaction, regardless of the profession.

My next key learning came from my experience with coaching the MBA students. Seeing how clueless they were when it came to figuring out what to work on solidified my belief that real change comes when a person knows exactly what their rough spots are. I decided everyone deserved access to specific feedback – not just executives.

Finally, my personal experience with 360-surveys guided my thinking on what would be really useful for helping people know about themselves. As an engineering manager in the mid-90's, I was subjected to a 360-survey. Many people would agree with me that 360-surveys are a harsh experience where feelings are hurt and nobody knows what the results really mean. A quick review of how people feel about 360-surveys rarely suggests that it is a positive experience.

In our company's process, my supervisor selected people who worked with me, and the system sent them a survey to fill out about my skills; I don't recall if I filled out a self-survey. At a general level, this survey provided feedback on communication, conflict resolution, and perhaps another seven typical categories of management and leadership. Anyway, the results showed that I had scores between 4 and 5 on a five-point scale for all categories except conflict. My conflict score was a 3.1. I was terribly upset by what I perceived to be a low score in conflict and asked my manager what the problem was. His reply was, "I don't know. I get along with you just fine. I'll go ask the people that filled out your survey and get back to you." I'm still waiting on him to get back to me...

Twenty years later, I still don't know what I needed to improve regarding my conflict skills, but my take-away from that experience is that people deserve to know exactly what they do well and what to improve. The Ambio360 shows you the average score for each individual skill and ranks those skills so you know where to start. Everyone deserves the details so they understand exactly where they stand.

You deserve to know what you do well and where you have opportunities to improve. As a part of this book, you have free access to an Ambio360 survey. The feedback you receive from the survey will provide a glimpse into how you stack up on the skills that have been reported to need the most work from our database of Ambio360 survey takers. It's a starting place for understanding your own unique skill set. You'll learn the details about how to get started on your own survey in the next section – Your Personal Ambio360.

Here's how the Ambio360 system of skills was created. From the research studies on Leadership, Management, and Performance, a list of over 350 specific skills was compiled to let people know how they stack up. Depending on your job and your place in life, some subset of these skills is crucial for Extraordinary Performance. The skills are packaged into sets that match up with your place in life. The Ambio360 Classic provides feedback on 125 basic skills that everybody needs, whether a teenager or a Vice President. The other Ambio360's check out skills based on your experience level (Young Professionals), your discipline focus (Technical Professionals), or your job (Program Manager or Manager).

I have been working with 360-surveys for over 15 years. My experience with the information learned from these surveys and from coaching people based on the feedback provided has taught me lessons. Hopefully, these lessons can help you decide if finding out how people really see your skills would also be helpful for you.

LESSON #1 – Without 360-feedback, people tend to work at getting better at what they are already good at, and completely ignore what they don't do well. Blind Spots are the skills we don't use. It's hard to work on something you don't even see. Most likely, if you could see what needs work, you'd already be fixing it. This misdirected focus to work on what you are already good at makes sense because we intuitively understand how to get better at something where we have a foundation. It is difficult to get started on learning a skill set where we don't even know the basics. The Ambio360 can let you in on your Blind Spots.

LESSON #2 – Once you see your feedback, you'll change whether you want to or not. One of my favorite stories about using the Ambio360 comes from a friend of mine. This lady is a successful sales representative for a difficult industry…merchant services (credit card service sellers). She took the Ambio360 and received negative feedback on several skills. She called me to complain that the system was wrong. She felt that she didn't need to change anything because she was successful. Her quote says it all:

"When I got my results, I thought that it was just who I was and I wasn't changing. Then, the next time I caught myself doing something I had received not-so-good feedback on, I stopped. I thought, I can find a better way. So, the bottom line is that this system helps you improve whether you want to or not."

LESSON #3 – You won't get very good information if you ask your friends and managers what they think about your performance. First, everyone else is not spending their day watching you so they can help you perform better. They are totally engrossed with just making it through the day themselves. So, you'll most likely get some random feedback that may or may not be accurate, and won't be specific. The first thing they think of will come blurting out.

For example, when you ask your manager how to be better, you may get a reminder that you were late yesterday...took too long for lunch last week...or missed a deadline last month.

In addition, most managers and friends don't know the list of 350 skills so they can evaluate you against that list. Given a list of items to watch for, people can provide accurate feedback; however, evaluating performance from a blank page doesn't provide feedback that pinpoints exactly what is working and what is not. The observers don't know what to look for.

LESSON #4 – People don't see their performance the same way others see them. Looking at the data from over 5000 users of the Ambio360, people rate themselves lower than others rate them over half the time.

It is as important to know what you do well as it is to know what to work on. The Ambio360 provides feedback on Master skills – or the skills that received an almost perfect score. When you embrace your Master-rated skills, you'll never doubt your judgment when you are called upon to use them.

YOUR PERSONAL 360-SURVEY

The Ambio360 survey provided with this book allows you to rate yourself on the top Needs Work items or *dings* reported across the general population. You can also send out email invitations to find out how others perceive you on these top problem skills. You'll be able to discover the skills others believe you do well and find out your top opportunities for improvement.

The Ambio360 Top 20 Dings is a short 20 skill survey is composed of the top 20 all-around reported skills that people need to work on. This survey is appropriate for all readers. The skills provide feedback in the areas of how you modify your behavior to work with others, competition, working in groups, and understanding others. The Ambio360 Top 20 Dings provides you feedback on:

COMMUNICATION
- Asking instead of Telling (Inquiry vs Advocacy)
- Asking Questions and Summarizing (Dynamic Listening)
- Being clear with what you say

DECISION MAKING
- Getting bogged down or rushing into decisions (Left Brain vs Right Brain)
- Separating facts from emotions

SELF MANAGEMENT
- Annoying behaviors such as sarcasm and harsh language
- Work/life Balance

WORKING WITH OTHERS
- Being too pushy or competitive
- Modifying who you are to better work with others

When you receive results and discover how others see your skills, you will be able to tailor your own personal plan for improving. You will understand what you do well in addition to the specific opportunities for improvement.

Even if you don't want to take the surveys, once you set up your account you'll have access to the online classroom that provides information about Best Practices associated with the skills in the survey, complete with online worksheets to guide your plan for improvement.

A STEP-BY-STEP GUIDE TO USING THE AMBIO360 SELF SURVEY

If you have never used a 360-survey, it can feel uncomfortable to ask people what they think about you. You might feel exposed. If you have never used a 360-survey or if you have had an unpleasant experience with one of these types of assessments, you'll most likely need to drum up a big dose of courage. However, the truth is that everyone already knows these things about you. They just don't have the words to let you know what you do well, and if you have some annoying habits, they most likely don't want to stir up any controversy by letting you know.

When most people get their results, their feedback indicates their skills are much better than they imagined. Then there are usually three or four things where they have room for improvement. Upon reflection most people say, "Yeah I knew that I was probably [annoying people/getting bogged down in the details/some other feedback item], but I was pretending it didn't really matter. Now I need to figure out a better way." You'll find that there are not really any secrets in your feedback. You are as good as you hoped you were, and deep inside, you already knew what you could improve.

Even if you are not interested in receiving feedback from other people, I encourage you to set up an account and at a minimum take the self survey. The questions in the self survey will help you start thinking about the most common problems that have been reported. Just seeing the questions and doing a self evaluation will start the process for improvement.

Also, once you set up your account, whether or not you take the self survey or ask others for feedback, you will have access to an online classroom that helps you understand best practices and more information on the top skills that are reported to need work. Using the survey takes five easy steps:

STEP 1: SET UP YOUR ACCOUNT. Go to www.ambio360.net/passkey. When you go to this webpage, the first question the system will ask you is to put in your passkey. The passkey is PB-2016.

Once you enter the passkey, you'll be asked if you already have an account. If you have used any Ambio360 survey in the past, enter your email address and password for that account and this survey will be added to the surveys you have already taken. If you have not used an Ambio360 before, you will be directed to the account setup page.

We do not share any of this information with anyone else. Please be careful to use an email address that is one you can actually get to as the system will be sending your reports to that email address. Once your account is set up based on an email address, it cannot be edited. This is the only piece of information that is fixed, so be careful to enter the email address that allows the system to communicate with you. All of the fields that must be filled in are indicated with an asterisk. If you are working on a tablet or small notebook, be sure to scroll to the bottom of the page and click that you agree with the Terms and Conditions.

Once your account is set up, you're ready to initiate the survey.

STEP 2: Now you are in the system and you will actually initiate your survey. If it is your first time to enter the system, you will be prompted you to take the self survey. If you take the self survey now, you will see the questions that other people will be asked if you decide to get feedback from others.

Once you have completed the self survey, you can always check on your self results. You do this by clicking on the Self bubble in the results table shown on the Results tab.

STEP 3: Once you have taken the self survey, the next step is to invite other people to provide feedback to you. Most likely you see the prompt that takes you to the page to send email invitations. However, from the dashboard or the menu bar you can select *Send Invitations* and you'll be taken to the screen where you input names and email addresses, along with how the person knows you, and they will be sent an email invitation as soon as you hit Submit upon entering their information.

Here are some tips about receiving quality feedback. Our research suggests that after about six people provide feedback, your results become stable. What we mean by stable is when somebody evaluates you as doing a skill Frequently, and someone else evaluates you as Always, that difference is just a matter of how people interpret frequently or always. Once six people have answered a question, the results settle out and become more useful. We recommend that you send a request for feedback to at least six people who have agreed to provide feedback, but to no more than 10 people.

In today's world of Internet spam and endless junk mail, you will need to let people know in advance that they will be receiving a *Request for Feedback* about you. Let them know that your goal is to learn what you do well and where you can improve. Most people are excited to help you out.

The best people to ask for feedback are those that know you well. The point is not to ask your enemy for feedback so you'll find more faults or to ask your best friend who would never say anything bad about you. Research has found that whether the people you ask are friends, enemies, family, or colleagues, people take this quite seriously and when answered honestly, the results always converge.

STEP 4: Now that you have completed the self survey and initiated emails requesting feedback, you'll receive your results when one of two conditions is met. Once 60% of your invitees have responded (as long as at least three people have responded), the system will show your results. The system waits three days to show results if less than 60% of your invitees have responded. After three days, if at least three people have responded, the system will show your results.

As soon as you have your results, the system will send you an email letting you know it's time to log back in to see your feedback.

STEP 5: Once your results are available, you'll be sent a link to a video that helps you debrief and understand what your results mean. The video takes you through how to think about feedback from other people and how to use the system's Work My Plan capability to help you create an action plan for improvement.

People get the most out of interacting with their results in the online system. You also have the option from the Dashboard to print reports that show your results.

THE ONLINE CLASSROOM

Another important feature of the online system is an interactive classroom. The classroom can be found under the Classroom tab when you log into your account on the Ambio360. The Classroom provides explanations and worksheets to help you understand more about how to develop the needed skills in the survey.

Whether you use the full system or just the parts that seem to work best for you, the purpose of the Ambio360 is to help you focus on how you improve. This system has been used extensively in corporations, leadership development for young managers in the military, and college students. Although it takes some courage to really look at yourself in the mirror that the feedback from others will provide, you'll make big improvements in a hurry once you know what to do.

To see our full range of 360-surveys, visit www.elaineseat.com.

REFERENCES

FUNDAMENTALS

THE PLAYBOOK

Developing Management Skills, 8th Ed, David A. Whetten and Kim S. Cameron, Chapter 3, provides a detailed analysis and approach to both analytic and creative problem solving techniques for managers.

BUILDING POSITIVE RELATIONSHIPS

INTRODUCTION

Developing Management Skills, 9th Ed, David A. Whetten and Kim S. Cameron, Chapter 4, provides the results of many studies on the necessity of communication skills for promotion and performance. Discussion of the research about how managers are not self-reflective is also provided, along with study citations that support this Introduction.

The discussion on Compassion comes from the *Oxford Handbook of Positive Organizational Scholarship*. 2012. Chapter 21: Compassion Revealed. Lillius, Jacoba; Kanov, Jason. Editors: Kim Cameron and Gretchen Spreitzer.

Gottman Relationship Blog: The Four Horsemen: Recognizing Criticism, Contempt, Defensiveness and Stonewalling, April 24, 2013; Ellie Lisitsa.

Making Relationships Work, A Conversation with John M. Gottman. *Harvard Business Review*, December 2007.

FYI: FI'S VS FD'S

Clark, S., Seat, E & Weber, F. (2000). The Performance of Engineering Students on the Group Embedded Figures Test, *Proceedings, Frontiers in Education Conference*, November, 2000. This paper documents simple testing of engineering sophomores to establish their high ability to dis-embed.

Witkin, Herman A. and Goodenough, Donald R. (1979). *Cognitive Styles: Essence and Origins, Field Dependence and Field Independence*. International Universities Press, Inc. New York. This book was published at the end of Dr. Witkin's life. In the Forward, he writes that the field is continuing to change. I have found this research helpful in explaining what I have seen in my work across disciplines.

Witkin, Herman A. and Goodenough, Donald R. (1977). Field Dependence and

Interpersonal Behavior. *Psychological Bulletin*, Vol 84, No 4, pp 661-689. This article is a summary of studies that describe differences in behaviors between Field Dependent and Field Independent persons. Details for the entries in Table 1 of this section were primarily derived from this article. The research on Looking Behaviors can be found starting on page 669.

Cameron, Kim (2013). *Practicing Positive Leadership: Tools and Techniques that Create Extraordinary Results*. Chapter 3 – How to Develop Positive Energy Networks.

Developing Management Skills, 9th Ed, David A. Whetten and Kim S. Cameron, Chapter 5, Table 5.2, Characteristics that Derail Manager's Careers. The authors provide credit to a study performed by the Center for Creative Leadership where 20 successful and 20 unsuccessful executives who began with equal promise were studied. The authors cite Psychology Today, 2006, www.psychologytoday.com as the basis for this information.

MATH OF THE EXTRAORDINARY

INTRODUCTION

Losada, M. & Heaphy, E. D. (2004). Positivity and Connectivity in the Performance of Business Teams: A Non-linear Dynamics Model. *American Behavioral Scientist*, 47, 740-765. This is the article about the 60 teams, and the intro quote.

Gottman Relationship Blog: The Positive Perspective: Dr. Gottman's Magic Ratio! December 5, 2012; Ellie Lisitsa.

Making Relationships Work, A Conversation with John M. Gottman. *Harvard Business Review*, December 2007.

SARCASM & CYNICISM

Oxford Handbook of Positive Organizational Scholarship, Positive Organizational Scholarship and Trust in Leaders. Mishra, Aneil & Mishra, Karen E.

Beck, Julie. 2013. How to Build a Happier Brain. *The Atlantic*, Oct 23, 2013.

The discussion on Resiliency comes from the *Oxford Handbook of Positive Organizational Scholarship*. 2012. Chapter 68: Resilience at Work. Brianna Barker Caza, Laurie P. Milton. Editors: Kim Cameron and Gretchen Spreitzer.

DELIVERING THE ONE

Cameron, Kim (2013). *Practicing Positive Leadership: Tools and Techniques that*

Create Extraordinary Results. Chapter 4 – Delivering Negative Feedback.

INQUIRY VS ADVOCACY

Losada, M. & Heaphy, E. D. (2004). Positivity and Connectivity in the Performance of Business Teams: A Non-linear Dynamics Model. *American Behavioral Scientist*, 47, 745-748.

CREATING EXTRAORDINARY PERFORMANCE

INTRODUCTION

Cameron, K. S., & Lavine, M. (2006). *Making the Impossible Possible.* San Francisco: Berrett-Koehler.

Wikipedia's write-up about what happened at the Rocky Flats Facility, https://en.wikipedia.org/wiki/Rocky_Flats_Plant

Hobbs, Ferrell P. (2011). *An Insider's View of Rocky Flats: Urban Myths Debunked.* Ferrell Hobbs worked at Rocky Flats before the FBI raid and afterward. He believes there was more criminal activity than just the handling of environmental waste. Whether you believe the urban myths or Mr. Hobbs' story of the poor handling of environmental waste, the incredible performance in the remediation project is the same.

USDOE Rocky Flats Project Office Closure Legacy – From Weapons to Wildlife. (2006). Available at http://rockyflats.apps.em.doe.gov

THE SWEET SPOT

Schmidt, Richard. (1988). *Motor Control and Learning*, pp 130-137. Discussion of Arousal, the Inverted-U, and Activation.

OBSTACLES TO CREATING EXTRAORDINARY PERFORMANCE

Industry-Specific Strategies of Winning Companies: An Analysis by Great Place to Work® (2015). Downloadable document.

Wanous, John and Austin, James. Academy of Management Best Paper Proceedings, 1994.

HARNESSING YOUR HORSEPOWER

CREATIVITY ON-DEMAND

Edwards, Betty. *Drawing on the Right Side of the Brain*, 4th Edition. 2012. Betty Edwards.

Seat, Janie Elaine (1996). *Women Engineers: Expectations and Perceptions.* Doctoral Dissertation. University of Tennessee, Knoxville. In this research, women engineers in the age group of 35-45 discussed how the best time of their career had been when they were working in a small group on a project. The group made friends, spent time together outside of work, and it was all driven by the creative synergy of co-working on a project together.

THE COACHING CONVERSATION

Cameron, Kim (2008) *Positive Leadership: Strategies for Extraordinary Performance.* Chapter 6. Discusses the value of on-going, regular, one-on-one meetings.

Tulgan, Bruce (2016). *Not Everyone Gets A Trophy: How to Manage the Millennials.* In this book Bruce Tulgan provides a kind way of understanding why the 35 and under crowd behaves as they do. Tulgan has a great section on why this generation needs coaching and how to have successful conversations. His work provided a starting point for the framework for the Coaching Conversation I describe.

USING THE AMBIO360™

Lesson #3 – Regarding how accurately people can evaluate others when given a list, please see the concluding section in *Blink* by Malcolm Gladwell, Chapter 1. In a summary of Rater Accuracy, Eichinger and Lombardo suggest that when people have known each other over three years and under one year, evaluation is not as accurate – with the group knowing each other one to three years being the most accurate in providing 360 feedback. The important point for our discussion is that feedback from others improves when they have a list of items to evaluate against rather than their own internal set of items. Fundamentally, people know how they experience someone, but do not know the specific skills and behaviors that create that perception.

McAnear, T. Paul & Seat, E. (2001). The Role of Peer Review in Engineering Task Teams. *Proceedings: Frontiers in Education Conference*, October 2001.

Seat, E. (2001). Administering, Scoring and Debriefing Team Developer. E. Seat. *Proceedings: Frontiers in Education Conference*, October 2001.

McAnear, P., Seat, E., & Weber, F. (2000). Predictors of Student Rating Accuracy. *Proceedings, Frontiers in Education Conference*, November, 2000.